ROBERT S. GRAHAM

J⦿B
KILLERS

The American Dream in Reverse

*How Labor Unions are Destroying
American Jobs and the Economy*

Tech PRESS
PUBLISHING

Paradise Valley • Arizona

IV : JOB KILLERS

Dedication

A special thanks to all of those who made this book possible, especially to the loves of my life – my wife Julia and my amazing children Robo, Jordan, Faith, Jackson and Reagan. I pray you will have the future America is capable of delivering.

This book is dedicated to the American workers who have sacrificed blood, sweat and tears to lift this great country to the top. May God bless each of you with opportunity, prosperity, good health and safety.

It's time to get it back.

Job Killers examines the role labor unions play on the American workforce, economy and livelihoods. For years, economists have conducted studies proving organized labor's adverse effect on America's businesses and workers. Through careful research and analysis, my book proves how labor unions are destroying American jobs and are keeping us from our right to work. *Job Killers* offers solid, results-based solutions to getting our country and economy back on track.

I'd like to thank Melissa Wenzel for her special contribution to *Job Killers*. Her hard work, professionalism and passion for the subject matter helped to move this project at an incredible pace. I would also like to thank my research team and sounding board Scott Titus, Brent Wadas, Matt Wharton, Mandy Morin and Ann Graham.

TABLE OF CONTENTS

Job Killers

The American Dream

Today's Entitlements are Tomorrow's Collapse

In all of my years of experience as a business/political leader, I've seen the American dream slowly but surely erode for most American families. There were days in America when a family could prosper from only one income and could depend on consistent work to provide a roof over our heads, a yard for our children and a safe neighborhood to come home to each evening. Those days are now disappearing right before our eyes.

The American dream has turned into a nightmare for most workers. Jobs are being exported overseas and layoffs are becoming more and more commonplace. Factories that were stalwarts of the Midwest have closed down. Entire towns that depended on American manufacturing for employment have become ghost towns; eerie reminders of dreams now dead, hopes now dashed. Indeed, the impossible has happened.

Companies that many saw as too big to fail have failed and those that still exist do so through risk and government promises. Throughout it all, few people have tried to answer the question; "how did this happen?" We need to learn from our mistakes and make America stronger for the future. That is what makes *Job Killers* such an important read for Americans today. *Job Killers* is able to statistically show the American dream is best served with free-market principles, not mandated labor costs and constraints on employers. Entitlement programs, the very programs fought for by union bosses for their members—have bankrupted companies—leaving the employees without jobs. No one had the courage to speak up in time to save hundreds of thousands of jobs—lost to other nations during the start of this young millennium. Today, we're seeing those same patterns emerging from programs run by our federal government.

From bailouts to handouts, we're seeing more and more American citizens and companies become contented, depending on the government for everything. In the meantime, our federal deficit grows and our debts mount. Eventually, a government that is supposed to be too big to fail will do just that – FAIL! and the devastation will be much more tragic than any of us can imagine.

Job Killers is not just another book railing about unions destroying free-market economies. It is a well-researched and a statistically supported argument that today's entitlements are tomorrow's collapse. The pathway to the American dream is paved in hard work and American determination—not forced membership and coerced entitlements.

Back on Track

Results-Based Solutions

A merica is in a critical state; truly in desperate need of resuscitation. Every day, businesses are losing millions of dollars to our global competitors. More and more Americans are finding pink slips where there should be paychecks. Never before has the American Dream been attacked as vehemently as it has during this "Great Recession."

While many culprits have contributed to this mess, one perpetrator plays a particularly damaging role in suppressing our country's ability to climb out of this recession – labor unions.

Growing up in the heart of the auto industry, in Michigan, I was well aware of the importance The Big Three played in our country's economy. I witnessed, firsthand, how American automakers provided for our neighbors and the dependence our state and nation had on a healthy auto industry. As I grew older, I learned about the underhanded politics and union bullying that has become more and more prevalent. What began as a movement to defend and protect the American worker has ended up costing them their jobs.

Labor unions are anything but a "Unified Voice." Instead, unions have caused the loss of American jobs and contributed to the downfall of our economy. Let me be clear. I have no qualms with unions that are able to organize within a company and work for the benefit of all involved. My problem lies with the unions that have stopped working for the employee and started working for themselves.

Unions are the *Mistletoe Effect* in its purest form. What may have started as a movement to unify workers, in the interest of establishing fair treatment and respectable wages, has turned into a survival story. Union organizations use questionable tactics to garner membership and exploit membership benefits in the name of "the worker." This parasitic practice is destroying the fabric of our country. Unions have invaded our way of life and have kidnapped the American Dream.

"Far better is it to dare mighty things, to win glorious triumphs, even though checkered by failure, than to rank with those poor spirits who neither enjoy nor suffer much, because they live in the gray twilight that knows neither victory nor defeat."

- Theodore Roosevelt

CHAPTER ONE

Unattainable or Forgotten

Why Americans Are Stumbling Off the Path to the American Dream

William Smith was just shy of his 19th birthday when he returned home to Maryland from the war. Returning home wounded from a mortar shell he sustained while taking cover in an irrigation ditch in Germany. His bright smile and shock of wavy black hair was a welcome sight to his family. William had witnessed some of the most difficult aspects of war and was eager to move on within the comforts of his beloved country.

William recalls reports of V-Day ringing through the radio while recovering in a hospital in England and a newly found optimism being shared amongst his comrades. People started smiling again as their hearts filled with feelings of hope and relief that the end of the war was near.

For William, life didn't stop upon his return home in 1945. Instead, it was just beginning. Serving his country and returning to the land he loved fueled his soul and inspired his desire to start his adult life. Upon completing high school, William wasted no time finding work and set out to achieve the American Dream – working hard to obtain a comfortable quality of life.

William grew up in what now would be considered a poor household. His parents owned their own business making souvenirs and paintings for tourists visiting Washington D.C. but struggled to make ends meet.

"My folks were hard working people. I was the youngest of six kids and recall a lot of hand-me-downs and meager meals. Even though they struggled financially, my parents instilled a sense of taking pride in one's work that I've carried with me my whole life." William said.

William's high school counselor recognized his talent for electrical work and machinery and recommended him for a job with a local hearing aid company.

William married his sweetheart Janet, built a home and started a family. He perfected his craft, and business was profitable and interesting. As word spread about his kind demeanor and impeccable craftsmanship, some of Washington D.C.'s most prominent public figures sought William's services, which kept him busy. Janet raised the family and kept his books while William worked long hours to put food on the table. After putting in 58 years of work with the same company, William and Janet retired and rescinded to the comforts of their home to enjoy their golden years. They had raised three sons and watched three grandchildren graduate from college – a luxury they never dreamed of for themselves. It wasn't always an easy life, but it was a successful life and for all intents and purposes, the American Dream was fulfilled.[†]

Formulating the American Dream, One Virtue at a Time

William is certainly not alone in his quest for the American Dream, nor is he the only one to have achieved it. The United States was built on the promise anyone can achieve the life we dream of — the American Dream.

The term, "American Dream", has varying interpretations, but is founded around upon the premise that through hard work, thrift and a healthy dose of optimism, a desirable quality of life is not only obtainable but is well within reach. Many also associate it with achieving a life better and easier than previous generations before them. Perhaps no one addressed the heart and soul of the American

Dream better than Abraham Lincoln. A true American success story and shining example of living the American Dream, Abraham Lincoln rose from the depths of poverty to become one of the most important and influential Americans of all time. He was brought up in poverty and experienced tragedy early in his childhood with the passing of his mother when he was ten years old. He struggled to feed his passion for learning in such destitute conditions; nonetheless, learned to read and write. He worked hard on his farm in New Salem, Illinois and gained experience in law before running for public office. Of his work ethic, his law partner once said of him, "His ambition was a little engine that knew no rest." His courage and tenacity led our nation through its most difficult period. Nothing but the pursuit of the American Dream, through hard work and optimism, could have prepared him better for such a difficult task. Anyone not experiencing such adversity, likely could not have handled the challenge and led our nation through the Civil War. Of pursing the American Dream, Lincoln once said,

"You can do anything you want – if you want it badly enough. You can be anything you want to be, do anything you set out to accomplish if you hold that desire with singleness of purposes."[†]

The term, "American Dream" was officially coined in 1931 by James Truslow Adams in his book, *The Epic of America*. According to Adams, the American Dream was the concept Americans, of any race and social rank, had the ability to achieve…a "better, richer and happier life." He wrote the American Dream, "is not a dream of motor cars and high wages merely, but a dream of social order in which each man and each woman shall be able to attain to the fullest stature of which they are innately capable, and recognized by others for what they are, regardless of the fortuitous circumstances of birth or position."[†]

Adams' description of the American Dream is the epitome of our nation's ideals — a Norman Rockwell painting in words.

The American Dream is unique to our country, not only in name, but in principle. No other country was built on such a solid foundation deeply rooted in protecting democracy and pursuing our dreams. It is a reason so many people immigrate to this country to experience a better way of life, one that is better than their parents'. The Declaration of Independence; the piece of writing that served as a pinnacle vow and testament for our country's democracy and independence, is exactly what the American Dream is all about. The declaration that "all men are created equal," and that they have "certain inalienable Rights" including "Life, Liberty and the Pursuit of Happiness" should be engrained in our minds and hearts.[†]

The American Dream encompasses how one perceives one's state of perfection, unique to each individual pursuing it. William Smith is not famous, nor is he considered wealthy, but what he achieved throughout his life is a successful, admirable achievement.

So with the American Dream within reach and deeply rooted in our nation's history, why are more people not able to achieve it?

In 2004, long before the Great Recession hit, a study conducted by KRC Research for the National League of Cities found two-thirds of Americans thought the American Dream was harder to achieve. The survey showed this to be especially true with young families. Aside from the September 11th attacks, when has our nation's youngest generations dealt with anything more severe or experienced a hardship greater than any of our previous generations, rendering them unable to achieve the American Dream? Is it unattainable or simply a lack of hard work and purpose?[†]

American Dream in Reverse –
Is the American Dream Still Alive?

The definition of the American Dream is shifting to an unfortunate new perspective. A combination of a culture change, coupled with economic hardship, has allowed people to forget what it means to be an American and what it takes to achieve success.

President Barack Obama, a shining example of the American Dream in action, has said the American Dream is "in reverse." Within days of taking office, President Obama faced a grim reality of a nation reeling in economic despair; the economy was shrinking, jobs were disappearing and unemployment was reaching highs unseen in a generation. Millions of American families were hanging on the hope President Obama, one man, would be able to turn their lives around. Responding to a report by the Commerce Department that the economy shrank further in the previous quarter, Obama said something many of us never thought they'd hear him say. On that cold Friday in January, President Obama, a man whose optimism and promise of a new day helped elect him president, told Americans the economy was a "continuing disaster for America's working families," a disaster that depicted an "American Dream in reverse."[†]

The American Dream *in reverse*. Going backward, undoing the hard work and successes we've accomplished along the way. The words seemed to hang in the air like lead balloons. And yet, we cannot deny the fact he may be right. No doubt, these are difficult times for Americans. Nearly everyone has been affected by the economy in some way or another and likely has experienced a backslide of their own goals and dreams. Retirement and savings accounts have shrunk, houses have been foreclosed, jobs have been lost and our spirit has been tested.

In his article, "Rethinking the American Dream," David Kamp describes the modern day American Dream and where it stands in our lives. "These are tough times for the American Dream. As the safe routines of our lives have come undone, so has our characteristic optimism – not only our belief that the future is full of limitless possibility, but our faith that things will eventually return to normal, whatever "normal" was before the recession hit."[†]

Has society given up on the American Dream? What led us to these horrible crossroads in our ideals as a nation and why, after centuries of success stories are people throwing in the towel on their American Dream?

Pipedreams and the Perception of
Easy Money for the *"ME"* Generation

In 2005, the Associated Press published an article labeling today's youth as the "Entitlement Generation." In it, the writer discussed how today's employers were dismayed with their young employees' demeanor and attitude; they expected too much, too soon. Many of these fresh faced employees have shockingly high expectations for salary, with little practical job experience. They want job flexibility and executive status but little willingness to take on grunt work or remain loyal to a company."[†]

As a business owner, I've run across this exact situation. Years ago, I hired a young man right out of college to an entry-level finance position. His resume consisted of little more than working at a fast-food restaurant and yet he was dismayed that I wanted to start him out at $28,000 per year. Gawking at my offer to pay him slightly over minimum wage, I explained to him he needed to prove his worth to me and actually earn the higher salary he expected. The young man accepted the terms and within 6 months, he doubled his income – he worked hard and proved his worth to me and my company. I learned very quickly that the new generation of workers now graduating college, is entering the work force with the perception of "entitlement first." This young man had the process of attaining a job *in reverse*, he cited online job resourcing sites, which displayed the "average" salaries new graduates were earning. His misperception – jobs were abundantly available and an employer, in this case, me, must maintain the averages and pay him more. However, as you can tell by his rapid increase in income, he demonstrated terrific value to our organization, and he EARNED the higher salary. His success was less about his "me" approach and became more about the value he brought to the organization.

I recently read an interesting book called, *Generation Me*, written by Jean Twenge, Ph.D., an associate professor of psychology at San Diego State University. Based on her years of research spanning 12 different studies on generational differences involving 1.3 million young people, she argues the generation of people born between 1979 and 1994 are the "Me Generation" – because of their impatient, self-serving tendencies and narcissism. Her book articulates the notion that today's young people are wrought with the entitlement perspective and inflated expectations.

Twenge writes, "Generation Mes' expectations are highly optimistic: they expect to go to college, to make lots of money, and perhaps even to be famous. Yet this generation enters a world in which college admissions are increasingly competitive, good jobs are hard to find and harder to keep, and basic necessities like housing and healthcare have skyrocketed in price. This is a time of soaring expectations and crushing realities."

Twenge feels the downfall of "GenMe" as she calls them, is not that they are spoiled or have it easy. In fact, it is quite the contrary when you consider today's youth face inflation, rising costs of childcare and cost of living along with tackling an increasingly competitive global marketplace. Rather, GenMe's downfall seems to lie with their upbringing and society's constant efforts to make sure everyone feels "special" and accomplished.

"GenMe has been raised thinking we were special and getting lots from Mom and Dad, but when we hit young adulthood we face an enormous mismatch between what we expect and what we actually get."[†]

While there are always exceptions, I believe today's workforce falls into a "meeting, not exceeding" category in the workplace. The danger of falling into this perception of entitlement is it enables laziness and can discourage innovation. This blasé approach to life stifles creativity and hard work – virtues our country desperately needs to recapture.

How quickly we've spiraled from the "Greatest Generation" to the "Entitlement Generation." Arguably, these narcissistic tendencies (or seemingly narcissistic) can simply be attributed to the rise in social networking along with the media's emphasis on celebrity and changing social norms. Regardless, the perception exists and it's time our nation's youth did something about it. We've suffered from a societal shift in expectations and output. Entitlement threatens productivity, success and innovation and it suppresses work ethic, a virtue our country needs to re-attain.

Pop culture and a societal shift in expectations and entitlement are chipping away at our moral fiber, misdirecting our need to work hard for a living. Instead of adhering to our nation's traditional values of hard work, many hope and wait for easy money. If we can't look like George Clooney or be born into money like hotel heiress Paris Hilton, we often feel the need to resort to other extremes to strike it rich in order to obtain their lifestyle.

In short, we've turned into a "get rich quick" society and the "work hard for what you have mentality" is hard to come by. Think about it – Americans get a daily dose of television ads encouraging taking legal action for a handsome settlement, reality and game shows award handsome sums of money to willing players, and state lotteries and casinos market the idea that you only need a buck and a dream to strike it rich. They all promise big money for little effort and we've fallen into the trap of believing we can actually do the same.

The increasing popularity of lotteries has proven more and more Americans pin their hopes on an empty promise of a pipe dream.

According to the National Gambling Impact Study Commission, lotteries are the most widespread form of gambling in the U.S. With 37 states and the District of Columbia operating lotteries, the Commission reports lotteries are the only form of commercial gambling in which a majority of adults report having played. State lotteries have the worst odds of winning (about 1 in 12-14 million) but they promise the biggest payoff with immediate gratification to the winners.

Lotteries also have the highest profits in the Unites States gambling industry. In 1996, the Commission reported $42.9 billion in total lottery sales, up 950% from 1982.[†]

Like labor unions, lotteries are notorious for preying on the lower-income groups through heavily funded, highly strategic marketing campaigns. Years ago, it became known the Ohio SuperLotto game's marketing plan targeted advertising days for the beginning of the month, timing its rollout to occur when Social Security checks and other benefits would be hitting mailboxes. It can certainly be argued this strategic scheduling preyed on a vulnerable population while generating millions of additional non-taxable funding.[†]

Promising players a way out of poverty, a controversial lottery ad campaign included a billboard in one of Chicago's poorest neighborhoods reading, "How to go from Washington Boulevard to Easy Street – Play the Illinois State Lottery."[†] Former California Governor George Deukmejian, an opponent of the lottery said, "I don't think it's good for the state or good public policy to go out and push and urge people to gamble."[†]

In 1984, a Gallup poll found that 20 percent of Americans agreed with the statement that the only way to get ahead is by playing the lottery.[†] Instead of pulling themselves up by their own bootstraps, down-on-their-luck individuals are encouraged to hang their hopes and few remaining dollars on the remote chance of winning a lottery instead of relying on hard work and dedication to improve their economic status.

Labor Unions:
Proponent of Entitlement

Even worse than the perception of entitlement or pie-in-the-sky notions of easy money, is an underlying force in our society that is systematically undermining our success. It is an institution so powerful and so deeply rooted in our workforce, its influence has been difficult to untangle. Labor unions are costing Americans their jobs and livelihoods, fundamentally unraveling the fabric of our country. What began as an admirable attempt to protect the American worker during the manufacturing era has become outdated and unnecessary in today's marketplace. With little to offer American workers by way of real, sustainable value, unions only serve to profit themselves and are chipping away at the pursuit of the American Dream in the process.

Bob Hagerty was an apprentice plumber in the early 1980s when he was hired to work on a commercial construction project in Plymouth, Minnesota. It was his first experience with labor unions and one he would not easily forget. The project entailed building an apartment complex and, as a plumber, Bob and his co-workers were tasked with installing new bathtubs throughout the multi-story complex. It was a laborious task to say the least. Because elevators had not yet been installed in the building, a journeyman and an apprentice had to haul the traditional-style bathtubs up four flights of stairs. Not only was the work backbreaking, it was time consuming as well.

One of the workers asked the petty bone lift operators (crane) to lift the tubs up for them. It worked brilliantly. Not only could they lift dozens of tubs at a time, saving them time and money, it was saving their bodies from difficult lifting.

Little did Bob know, the backbreaking work wasn't over. In fact, it hadn't begun.

"One of the union stewards found out about our operation and stopped it immediately," Bob recalled. "He said it wasn't in the lift operator's duties and made us haul every single bathtub out of the building only to turn around and take them back upstairs again by hand. The union's interests were only in milking the time it took to complete the job, completely disregarding efficiency. What originally took us a day to complete with the lift, ended up taking us more than three weeks to haul the tubs up to the apartments."

Bob recalled several other examples of unions implementing unnecessary rules and procedures in order to prolong the job. In fact, Bob's boss was forced to declare bankruptcy at the end of the project because it dragged out so long.[†]

This is just one example of how unions are driving companies out of business and instilling a manipulative and lazy mentality in our country's workers.

While unions claim their members receive higher wages than non-union members, the fact remains the money needs to come from somewhere…or rather someone. Most often that "someone" is you, the consumer. Most Americans are under the delusion the extra wages given to union members comes out of the business owner's pockets, but, it does not. Most likely it is the consumers who pay higher prices when companies are faced with making up the difference and maintaining a profitable bottom line. Unions drive up the cost and consumers are faced with paying higher prices. When they do not (or can't), the company's profit is lowered, workers are laid off and the downward spiral continues. In today's economic climate, such a parasitic scenario is devastating to our workforce and our livelihoods as Americans.

Through effective legislation and labor laws, labor unions have become a parasite on our nation's economy, feasting on our successes and work ethic. Unions are leading to the downfall of the American Dream and American's right to work. They are the ultimate job killer. Unions are taking American workers from the picket lines to the unemployment lines. Their "Unified Voice" misleads Americans into thinking they have the workers' best interests at hand. But, their unified voice is no longer strong and protective. It has evolved into a voice that is overbearing, controversial and irrelevant. For an organization who claims to speak for so many, why are so many people questioning it?

We must ask ourselves: will we lose the American Dream so long as unions are allowed to degrade our values? I say yes.

† See appendix for reference.

*"The trees, through summer, yet forlorn and lean,
O'ercome with moss and baleful mistletoe."*
*– The Lamentable Tragedy
of Titus Andronicus
William Shakespeare*

CHAPTER TWO

The
Mistletoe Effect

The Promise That is Destroying America

Hung joyfully in doorways and from mantels in winter, mistletoe brings with it tidings of peace and love as we kiss and embrace beneath it. Throughout civilization, mistletoe has carried with it enormous cultural and mythological symbolism. In ancient Greece, it was recognized as a symbol of the birth of the New Year and ancient Romans believed it to be a source of good fortune. The Druids called it "the Golden Bough," believing it so sacred it was never allowed to touch the ground. The Welsh considered it pure gold, directly from the sun. Scandinavian mythology recognizes mistletoe as the plant of peace. If Scandinavian enemies met beneath a bough of mistletoe, they were to lay down their arms and call a truce until the next day. And it appears ancient Celts believed mistletoe to be endowed with mystical healing powers. Throughout history, it has been thought to promote fertility and prosperity and even in recent history, it has been used as a homeopathic treatment for cancer and AIDS.

Yet little of the playful mysticism we ascribe to mistletoe bears the truth of this celebrated plant. In fact, as Shakespeare wisely illustrates in his tragic play *Titus Andronicus*, mistletoe is a parasite that slowly, willingly kills host shrubs and trees. More than 1,300 species of mistletoe exist today, all of which thrive by robbing food and water from host plants. After the mistletoe seed is driven into the ground, it drives its roots deep into the woody structure of the host's stem, melding with and becoming a living part of the host. This enables it to draw sap and nutrients from the host, thereby killing it. As a matter of fact, mistletoe is thought to be an herbal remedy, even though most species' berries are poisonous to animals and it has been found in large doses to be toxic.

The irony of mistletoe reveals a greater truth: sometimes, the things we believe in most, those things that seem to offer us the most promise, can ultimately be our downfall. Furthermore, because of our stubborn desire to hang onto those beliefs, we often refuse to recognize the problems that come as a result, so the problems continue to grow. This is what I call the Mistletoe Effect.

So what does this have to do with American industry and labor unions? Consider how unions developed and what they have become.

When colonists settled the New World, they did so with the hope that with hard work, anything was possible. They sought opportunities that had long since dried up in the Old World. So, many of them entered into indentured servitude as a way to earn passage to America. Upon arriving here, this land of promise, they were bound to many years of unpaid labor as they repaid their debts for passage.

As Americans increasingly sought their independence from Britain, the interests of workers became even more important. The Boston Massacre was born out of a disagreement between Boston ropemakers and off-duty soldiers who were making rope on the side to supplement their income. These disgruntled ropemakers, angry over issues of unfair competition, led a worker uprising eventually sparking talk of a revolution. It was during this time workers began uniting; finding strength in numbers as they negotiated with employers for proper treatment and fair pay. The United Company of Philadelphia for Promoting American Manufacturing unified 400 women—in New York City journeyman printers united to gain an increase in wages, and shoemakers went on strike for three weeks. Shortly afterward, in

Philadelphia, carpenters went on strike for higher pay and shoemakers formed the first local craft union for collective bargaining. Unification of workers, it seemed, was becoming an antidote to the unfair treatment propagated by wealthy employers.

The Industrial Revolution brought with it further unionization, as the United States population grew at a staggering rate and the workforce nearly tripled in size. Workers struggled continuously to ensure safe working conditions, reasonable compensation and fair treatment by employers. Upton Sinclair's landmark book, *The Jungle*, exposed the unsafe, unclean conditions in the Chicago meatpacking industry, bringing further scrutiny to labor practices. Unionization, it seemed, was the only way to ensure workers would be treated fairly. Workers labored for better wages, benefits and work environments. As a result, labor laws were put into place, such as those related to the 8-hour workday or the minimum wage and the U.S. Department of Labor was established.

In essence, the American worker could begin to expect fair and equitable treatment on the job and American industry began to thrive with a happier workforce. The United States became the most important country in the world. American businesses became a shining example to the world of the power of the common man.

The problem employers have over time, is to adopting long-term goals that include maintaining high quality employees through offering a combination of fair wages and good working conditions. It's no longer necessary to unionize to ensure workers will have a safe place to work or enough time off; the U.S. Department of Labor and OSHA see to that. In fact, the success of unions has been their demise. Yet, unions continue to push the adoption of high-cost benefits, which, over time, has significant, irreversible impacts on not only business owners but ultimately on workers and individual states.

What may have started as a movement to unify workers, to establish fair treatment and respectable wages, has turned into a survival story. Union organizations exploit membership benefits and the "for the worker" approach (in parasitic fashion) to eventually suck dry the very businesses – and by extension, the workers – they were originally formed to prop up (the "hosts"). Under the guise of benefiting workers and businesses, this group mentality distorts reality, confusing *want* with *need*, as the parasite uses the host to thrive and secure gain. This is the Mistletoe Effect resulting in tremendous cost.

Today we find ourselves in dire circumstances financially. At the time of this writing, the Congressional Budget Office estimates that the current U.S. output is $1 trillion below its potential, and unemployment reached a 68-year high, the worst it's been since the Great Depression. In the midst of a disastrous time for the country's auto makers, when the industry is fighting to stay alive, United Auto Workers union members make, in salary and benefits, $73 per hour – a full $30 per hour more than Toyota plant workers.

What's wrong with this picture? Surely, this country's earliest unionists did not envision organizations that would tear at the roots of the businesses they supported and worked hard to make successful.

No one is here to argue the role unions played in the evolution of this country. And while, of course, the history of right-leaning opposition to unions is long and storied, it's also worth considering unions may have fulfilled their purpose, and at this stage in our history, they are doing more harm than good.

---

† *See appendix for reference.*

"There was no precise moment when the tide began to turn against labor unions in America. There was no single catastrophic event -- no landmark strike that was broken, no massive organizing campaign that was turned back, no key negotiation that went poorly for labor. But beyond any doubt, since the early 1980s, unions have lost many of their resources and much of their influence."

– Gary Chaison
Unions and Legitimacy

Labor Unions

The History and Resulting Impact

Labor unions, in the United States, have become a national establishment. Their story is one filled with triumph and tragedy, advancement and corruption. Labor unions played an important role in our nation's history and while their current-day relevance is disputed, their significance in our nation's economy and workforce should not be denied. What began as an admirable attempt to protect the American worker has become outdated and unnecessary in today's marketplace. Through effective legislation and labor laws, labor unions have priced themselves out of the market and are leading to the downfall of the American Dream.

Labor unions are organizations that play an intermediary role between worker and employer in negotiating wages, benefits and work conditions. There are trade unions that represent workers who do a particular job and industrial unions, which represent workers in a particular industry. While history of labor unions, in our country, is traced back to our earliest days of settlement, the philosophy behind American labor unions arose out of the manufacturing era when bargaining tactics and protecting the common worker were needed. The manufacturing industry was a large producer in America's economy from the 1930s through the 1960s and there is little denying the fact unions played a key role in ensuring the fair treatment and compensation of America's working class.

Pushed to the Brink

Perhaps the earliest rumblings of organized unions are traced back to the Colonial Era with the conflict of the Boston Massacre in 1770. A clash between British soldiers and civilians resulted in the deaths of five civilians, highlighting the problem of rising taxes and stifling laws set forth by the British Parliament. Bostonians had reached their limit with the King's rule and took their frustrations out on a lone British sentry patrolling his post in front of the Custom House. A group of men and boys taunted the young soldier until alarm bells rang in the streets, indicating trouble. A crowd descended upon the scene bringing with it panic and melee. Defending the soldier were eight British redcoats; bayonets fixed and ready. As the crowd grew louder, one of the British soldiers opened fire. Chaos ensued with five men dying as a result and escalated tension between countries.[†] In short, the citizens of the New World had enough ill-treatment and were being pushed to the brink of their tolerance for British rule. In fact, it can be argued the Boston Massacre, and the unionized spirit in which it was enacted, was the straw that broke the camel's back leading to the American Revolution and, ultimately, our country's freedom. The Boston Massacre resembled a Progressive Era labor dispute and got results. On that cold winter night in 1770, the group of Bostonians found empowerment in their unified voice – an action millions of Americans would duplicate throughout history.

As America matured as a nation and found its economic footing, the issue of labor found its way back into the forefront of industry and politics. During the 1790s, unions were most often organized by skilled workers, advocating reform within their particular trade. Most often, they were small groups formed to organize and carry out a particular strike and disbanded afterwards.

The National Trade Union was the first nationwide organization to form in 1834 but due to a variety of factors such as the economic crisis of 1837 and the depression that followed, membership stalled.[†]

Strength in Numbers: Unions Find Their Footing

The period between the end of the Civil War through the 1890s, Americans settled 430 million acres in the West – more land than during the entire 250 years prior. With this tremendous land expansion also came tremendous growth – especially in the transportation and manufacturing industries. This growth, coupled with technological advances lead to significant economic growth in the United States. The expanding railway and canal system made transportation quicker and more efficient. Inventions such as electricity, the telephone and Eli Whitney's cotton gin also helped Americans churn out more products even faster. Spurred on perhaps, by the allure of money, Americans invented a multitude of ingenious gadgets, tools, equipment and communications devices during this time period. Frederich Engels, a German social scientist, called it America's "energetic, active population." Between 1790 and 1810, the United States government issued an average of 77 patents to citizen inventors each year. In 1830, the number of patents jumped to 544 and by 1860, it rose to a whopping 4,778. According to historians, during most of this time period, the United States granted more patents than England and France combined.[†]

In what should have been an economic boom for Americans, was indeed not. The facts around America's financial successes were deceiving. Such growth and prosperity did not trickle down to the workers whose long hours of arduous work did little to ease their economic suffering. The country's wealth remained in few pockets while workers suffered from little pay, long hours and deplorable conditions. Such a contradiction in America's social standings led to great divides between the elite and the working class. This era became known as the Gilded Age, a term coined by authors Mark Twain and Charles Dudley Warner in their novel, *The Gilded Age: A Tale of Today*.

Twain and Warner viewed the present-day dynamic as "gilded" – beautiful on the surface but cheap and tarnished underneath.[†] America, the land of opportunity, was only rewarding a select few – the Robber Barons, as they became known, and seemingly punished those actually doing all of the work and labor for them. Robber Barons were American capitalists in the late 19th century who became wealthy through the exploitation of others.[†]

Twain and Warner's description of the country was impeccable. People such as John D. Rockefeller, J.P. Morgan and Cornelius Vanderbilt profited enormously in these years, building gigantic mansions, engaging in lavish spending and living in the lap of luxury – all on the backs of the working class. These Robber Barons often participated in unethical and manipulative business practices.[†] The Gilded Age was the *Mistletoe Effect* in its purest form – a seemingly beautiful economic system being disguised as truly profitable and beneficial to the country as a whole. What it was really doing was poisoning America's largest population – the working class. These merchant princes sucked the life out of America's workers, all the while profiting enormously at their expense. But this is America after all, and like the spirit in which our forefathers fought for our independence, the workers rose up to take responsibility for their own well being. Hence, the modern-day labor union was born.

The significant divide between the upper and working classes, coupled with the long hours and hazardous conditions that were commonplace in American industry in the late nineteenth century, helped lead America down a path to unionization. As America's largest industries found ways to cheaply pump out more consumables, laborers suffered. Fed up with conditions, workers sought to better their lives by taking matters into their own hands. Finding strength in numbers, workers formed unions to help leverage better working conditions and compensation. Numerous attempts at unionizing in these early days resulted in both outstanding successes and resounding defeats.

The first national union to form was the National Labor Union

(NLU) in 1866. Within two years of its organization, the NLU had more than 600,000 members. As the NLU grew, it took on an agenda broader than economic and working conditions. Their new platform involved politics which, inevitably, alienated hundreds of its members. The withdrawal of these members ultimately led to the NLU's collapse in 1872.[†]

The creation of the NLU was followed closely by the formation of the Knights of Labor union in 1869. Its organization encouraged the participation of workers from virtually all trades. The Knights of Labor operated as a secret society in its early years before expanding so vastly. Soon the secret and mystique of the organization was eliminated at which point it began operating like a traditional trade union. A number of reforms were advocated, such as the establishment of the eight hour work day, equal opportunities of wages for women and regulations against child labor. The Knights of Labor enjoyed some success such as playing a vital role in the strikes by coal miners and railroad workers in 1877 before dissolving in 1917.

Labor finally seemed to find its footing with the establishment of the American Federation of Labor. The AFL, led by Samuel Gompers, united an estimated 316,000 workers grouped in 25 national unions of various trades. Differing from the Knights of Labor, the AFL maintained autonomy in dealing with the trades – each union retained exclusive rights to work with its own unions and workers within each field. Instead of campaigning for sweeping reform like the Knights of Labor, the AFL centered its advocacy on the pursuit of specific goals such as obtaining higher wages and establishing shorter hours for its workers. Interestingly, the AFL encouraged its members to support political candidates friendly to the union movement rather than endorse a particular political party.[†] Gompers served as president of the AFL, with the exception of one year, from its inception in 1886 until his death in 1924.[†]

After years of hard work, the 1890s rewarded the unions with the establishment of an eight-hour work day. The years that ensued were difficult for unions as they continued fighting the employer establishment and suffered from failed strikes and a contracting economy.[†] The country was experiencing an evolving ideology as it related to capitalism and labor conflict. As industry progressed, the unions once again rose to the occasion and reestablished their presence in America's workplace.

War, Depression and Advances:
A Period of Great Transition for Labor

The 35 years following the end of the Civil War to the beginning of a new century was a period of prosperity, coupled by crushing defeats for unions. By the end of World War I, the United States had risen to become one of the top-seeded world powers. The United States experienced an explosion of industry and production as coal mining, railroads, steel mills, factories and communication advances took effect. In fact, at the beginning of the 20th century, per capita income and industrial production in the U.S. exceeded that of any other country in the world, except Britain.[†] For all intents and purposes, the United States should have been a prosperous, healthy nation. It was not. Instead, it was on the brink of collapse and its working class was sick with poverty and unsightly working conditions.

The new century brought turmoil and disputes between employers and workers more than ever before. By 1904, more than two million workers were members of unions and nearly 1.7 million belonged to the AFL. Women began joining unions and many industries such as publishing, construction and railroads, began accepting union influence and negotiations as the norm. This time period is where unions found a truly passionate voice with a strong, organized following.

Arguably, some of the most important strides made by the unions during this time period were in Congress. In 1913, the United States Department of Labor was created, cementing the issue of labor as a top-tiered priority on a national level. Massachusetts became the first state to enact the first minimum-wage law in the U.S. and World War

I provided opportunities for increased recognition with the reliance on workers and factories producing materials to win the war. By 1920, trade unions boasted a membership of 5.1 million members; more than 80 percent of them belonging to the AFL.[†]

Navigating Unstable Ground

Labor unions became more and more active in the years following the war. Between 1914 and 1920, unions averaged 3,000 strikes per year.[†] Activism also saw unions suffering several crushing defeats in the years that followed; namely a failed iron and steelworker strike in 1919. The iron and steel companies refused to negotiate with the unions and an industry-wide strike was organized in September, 1919. It became one of the largest strikes in history involving approximately 370,000 workers. Disorganization within the union ultimately led to the workers' defeat without earning any concessions from the employers. The result of this strike left its effects on the union for years to come as the iron and steel industry remained an "open shop" industry, meaning union membership would not be mandatory and it remained this way for nearly two decades.

The United States suffered a grim post-war depression from 1921 to 1922 resulting in a decline in union membership and participation. The rise in unemployment led to a decline in membership and promises of better wages to workers. Union membership dropped from 5.1 million members in 1920 to 3.5 million in 1929. The Great Depression would only deepen the wound for unions until President Franklin Roosevelt would come to their rescue with New Deal legislation.

The New Deal, as it became known, was enacted and passed by President Roosevelt and members of Congress for the purpose of stimulating the economy and labor during the Great Depression. These series of economic laws and programs, passed between 1933 and 1935, focused on the "3 R's" – providing *relief* to the unemployed; particularly suffering farmers, *reform* of business practices and promoting economic *recovery*. In the second wave of New Deal legislation, as it related to labor, part of the efforts included the formation of the National Industrial Recovery Act (NIRA) in June, 1933. The Act was riddled with controversy as it stipulated "employees have the right to organize and to bargain collectively through representatives of their own choosing and shall be free from the interference, restraint, or coercion of employers…in the designation of such representatives." Unions wasted little time taking advantage of this and organized workers in various industries, boosting the AFL's 2.5 million members to more than 3 million. In May, 1935, the United States Supreme Court deemed the NIRA unconstitutional.[†]

Senator Robert F. Wagner was a particularly active voice in Congress during this time. He believed the current labor dispute system, under the NIRA, was extremely flawed. In his view, the suffering American economy would not be fixed until a revitalized labor movement was established that could legitimately protect workers' rights. He also believed that through strong labor unions, increasing wages for workers would serve as the ultimate economic stimulus.

Wagner and members of Congress reformulated its philosophical foundation by enacting the National Labor Relations Act (NLRA), or commonly known as the Wagner Act, which exemplified the current administration's strong commitment to organized labor. The Act reinstated workers' rights to organize freely, encouraged collective bargaining and increased penalties to employers who interfere with organization efforts. The Wagner Act also made financial support or domination of unions by employers illegal which essentially eliminated company-run employee associations that had previously formed.[†] Perhaps one of the most significant issues to come out of the Wagner Act was the shift it caused in the manner disputes were enacted and handled. Prior to the act, strikes and disputes were often violent where hundreds of workers died and thousands more suffered serious injury. The Wagner Act was successful in encouraging disputes to be handled in meetings and courtrooms versus the streets and alleyways.[†]

The Wagner Act would subsequently be amended with the passage of the Labor Management Relations Act of 1947, better known as the Taft-Hartley Act. The Act served as a watchdog over union activities. It placed several restrictions on unions including limiting their right to strike and revamping the National Labor Relations Board. Senator Robert Taft and Representative Fred Hartley, Jr. championed the Act, hoping it would stabilize the debilitating effects the Wagner Act had on America's business landscape. Taft said he hoped the Act would "restore some equality between employer and employee so that there might be collective bargaining."[†] As a whole, the bill's sponsors hoped the Act would discourage frequent strikes and would protect workers and employers alike from so-called "wrongdoing" that was so frequently decried by unions. Overall, through the appointment of a brand new NLRB, the Taft-Hartley Act aimed at striking a balance between worker and employer by way of a neutral entity, or as Representative Hartley called it, a "referee."[†]

The Congress of Industrial Organization (CIO) formed in 1935, uniting the iron and steel, automobile, rubber, radio, shipping and electric industries and was quick to become successful in instituting so-called "sit-down strikes" which involved striking workers occupying the plants during their disputes.

Congress' enactment of the NLRA gave the union movement momentum in organizing and recruiting members. By 1945, union members totaled approximately 14 million, making up about 35 percent of the civilian workforce.[†]

At Odds with General Motors

Following World War II, the United Automobile Workers, through the CIO, enacted the first, largest and longest post-war strike which lasted from November 1945 thru March the following year. Their demand was slightly different from their other strikes – this one involved negotiating higher wages for their members without raising the price of automobiles. General Motors refused to negotiate prices but it could be argued this first strike paved the way for future demands made upon automobile makers. In fact, in June of 1955, union members won a huge battle with automakers by securing a guaranteed-wage plan under which members were eligible to receive a higher compensation during periods of unemployment.[†]

A Marriage of Two Unions

Starting in the 1950s, American wealth began experiencing an interesting shift from a struggling working class to more affluent one. According to *American Workers, American Unions*, the decades "between 1950 and 1970 saw the United State's real gross national product expanded by $350 billion in which real weekly earnings for production workers leapt 70 percent." Home ownership expanded and an increasing number of households were comprised of two-income families. Approximately 60 percent of American families were now listed in "middle class" income brackets.[†]

In December 1955, in an effort to build a strong coalition and bolster a slumping public opinion of unions, the AFL and CIO merged to become the American Federation of Labor and Congress of Industrial Organizations. Subsequently, a series of audits and ethical standards programs revealed evidence of widespread corruption, particularly with the Teamsters Union, to which the AFL-CIO expelled them from their union. The following years would find the AFL-CIO at odds with one another within their ranking leaders as issues such as civil rights failed to be communicated and properly addressed.

The 1980s found the AFL-CIO with slumping membership and a mere one-sixth of the labor force in the United States were card-carrying members. Issues that plagued unions included the outsourcing of jobs overseas where wages were much more affordable to companies, a general lack of interest in union representation among younger workers and the apparent erosion of unions' effectiveness at the bargaining table.[†]

Today, according to the AFL-CIO, approximately 15.4 million

workers belong to unions with 11.5 belonging to the AFL-CIO which is comprised of 57 different union divisions. The AFL-CIO also says union workers earn 30 percent more each week than nonunion workers and are much more likely to have health and pension benefits.[†]

Grasping at Straws – Unions' Recruitment Tactics

There is little doubt labor unions played an important role in our country's economy. As we've discussed, without them, the United States would likely have remained stuck in the Gilded Age with a downtrodden workforce working their fingers to the bone to line the pockets of a small group of Americans. In the 1950s, approximately one-third of American workers belonged to unions. Today, despite pricey recruitment campaigns, unions have struggled to eek out a slight increase in membership, reversing a 25-year downward trend. That "increase" was slight. According to a report issued by the Bureau of Labor Statistics, membership of employed workers went from 12.1 percent in 2007 to 12.4 in 2008.[†] To put it in perspective, in 1983, approximately 20 percent of U.S. workers were members of unions.[†]

Unions, such as the AFL-CIO, continue to pledge to get members higher wages, benefits and job security but present day issues have made that promise difficult – if not impossible – to keep, thereby rendering them ineffective. In short, labor unions' role has changed. Having accomplished as much as they have, specifically in the way of labor laws and standards, they have virtually priced themselves out of business. Their mission has become obsolete and their relevance in today's marketplace is questionable. In recent years, their legal entanglements and infighting has cost them the trust and confidence of their members and, like a sinking ship, many unions are searching for a life preserver, clinging to whatever rules and regulations they can impose on American businesses just to stay afloat. All of this is done at the expense of businesses. Their mission today – is a parasite to the millions of business owners struggling to earn a profit in a competitive and tough economic environment. As we'll learn, unions cause job losses, discourage investment and serve as a lead weight to the businesses and industries that keep our great country afloat in a difficult economy. Recent union strong-arming in Congress, such as the so-called Employee Free Choice Act, only solidify how far the apple has fallen from the tree. Numerous studies performed by economists from around the world confirm what many in business have been feeling for a long time – unions are bad for business, bad for American jobs and bad for our economy.

"Labor unions would have us believe that they transfer income from rich capitalists to poor workers. In fact, they mostly transfer income from the large number of non-union workers to a small number of relatively well-off union workers."

         – Robert E. Anderson
         Just Get out of the Way

CHAPTER FOUR

Decay in Today's Economic Climate and Marketplace

As we've learned, unions serve as a third-party "negotiator" between worker and employer. Their role, they say, is to secure fair wages, safe work environments and adequate health benefits for their members. Like the mistletoe, on the surface, it sounds great, but underneath, their system is tearing apart our economy. By demanding higher wages and benefits from employers already struggling to turn a profit, they are shoving our country's businesses into the difficult position between a rock and a hard place.

Additionally, as our country has evolved, so have the needs in the marketplace. Assembly lines occupied by thousands of workers were replaced with automated machinery and solely run by computers. The idea that America's largest production lines needed to get able bodies into their factories to work (regardless of talent, education or skill level), slowly melded into today's need for skilled, motivated workers.

This shift in America's workforce and the passing of effective labor laws in Congress contributed to the decrease in union membership. We simply don't need them. Infighting among union bosses and a declining public perception of their effectiveness also contributed to the downfall of unions. In fact, since their heyday in the 1950s, unions have generally reported a steady decrease in private sector membership and representation across the United States.

The Perfect Storm: The Downfall of The Auto Giants

Great minds, like Benjamin Franklin and Abraham Lincoln, have said industry is the key to achieving success – but only if it is executed correctly. General Motors is a perfect example of how devastating unions can be for the economy, killing thousands, if not millions of U.S. jobs. It is reported that United Auto Workers (UAW) earn an average of $75 per hour in wages and benefits. This is nearly triple the earnings of the average worker in the private sector. (Sherk, James) The bloated benefits, coupled with the JOBS bank that pays UAW workers nearly their full wages when they've been laid off, have been a driving force leading to the downfall of GM's corporate structure; threatening their survival.

In what should have been a very exciting and profitable year for GM, 2008 it turned into a nightmare. GM found themselves closing factories, laying off workers and filing for bankruptcy. Perhaps the strongest example of GM's downfall against its competitors lies in the numbers. Just one year earlier, in 2007, GM and Toyota sold about the same number of cars but their profit margins differed wildly. GM, selling 9.37 million vehicles (GM.com) recorded a profit/loss of $-38.7 billion, or about $4,055 per car.[†] Toyota, on the other hand, also sold roughly 9.37 million and made approximately $15 billion.[†] Why the massive difference in profit? ...Overhead! Toyota, a foreign entity, doesn't have to deal with the labor union issues and payouts like GM.

David Cole, Chairman of the Center for Automotive Research attributes the GM meltdown to a number of contributing factors: the economy, a general lackluster product-line of cars and legacy costs. Every single car GM makes has an additional $2,000 tacked onto its sticker price to cover 'legacy costs'; costs to provide benefits and healthcare to GM's retired workers and their families.[†] Not only are they unable to lower this $2,000 markup, GM is forced to compete with foreign automakers such as Toyota and Honda who don't have any of these costs to pass onto the consumer. Domestic car companies simply cannot compete with foreign companies if they are forced to contend with labor unions strong arming them into passing on the extra fees to the consumer. The Auto Giants (GM and Chrysler) begged Congress for a financial bailout so they could attempt to crawl out from the tremendous hole they've dug themselves into. Instead of filing for bankruptcy, which would allow them the necessary tools to restructure their broken companies and free up some of their contractual obligations, they asked the taxpayers to ease their load; a load that includes paying for some of the most highly-paid workers in the country. That's not to say, of course, that retirees don't deserve healthcare and benefits, but when one of the biggest auto giants in the world is going under, closing factory doors and laying off its workers and legacy costs and inflated wages are the biggest reasons why; it's time to reevaluate the system.

According to the article written by James Sherk for the Heritage Foundation, reporting on analysis performed by the U.S. Department of Labor, the average hourly compensation (which includes wages and benefits) paid to America's private sector employees totaled $25.36 per hour. Workers at Japanese auto plants located in the United States earned between $42 and $48 per hour (approximately $80,000 per year) and in 2006, the average UAW worker at the Big Three earned between $71 and $78 per hour. What do these outrageous wages equate to? Unionized workers at the Big Three earn an average $130,000 per year in wages and benefits.

The Heritage Foundation research acknowledged that a significant percentage of UAW member earnings come in the form of benefits. They cited approximately 38 percent of the $75.81 an hour wage that Chrysler's UAW workers earned came as base wages. That said, they also pointed out UAW workers get, what they called, "gold-plated health care." The UAW negotiated above-average health benefits to their members and families with low monthly premiums of $10 for an individual and $21 for families. Coverage also includes things such as hearing aids, dental and even Lasik eye surgery.[†]

UAW workers and their pensioned employees are receiving some of the best and least expensive health care in the country – all at a time when millions of Americans either can't afford health care or pay out of their pockets for minimal and often substandard coverage.

In 2007, *Fortune* magazine published an article in a 2006 report prepared by Harbour-Felax, a Detroit-area consulting firm. The firm found labor costs, and more specifically health care costs, to be one of the most arduous issues plaguing the Big Three. They found GM spends $1,635 per vehicle on health care for active and retired workers in the United States. Toyota, on the other hand, pays nothing for retired workers and only $215 for active workers. Tack on an additional $630 per vehicle to account for union imposed labor costs such as: contractual issues and rules, line relief and holiday pay – costs the Japanese automakers simply don't have. Paying UAW workers for *not working* when plants are shut down adds another $350 per vehicle as well.[†]

The American Dream is attacked on both sides of the issue – the workers being laid off, the executives at the top are put in a position of great financial hardship *and* the reverse — retirees losing benefits. This is yet another example of setting the American Dream in reverse, and how unions are killing American jobs.

"Cartel"-like Actions Characterize Today's Unions

The Heritage Foundation, a public policy research think tank, acutely describes labor unions as "cartels" because their actions limit the number of workers in a company; ultimately driving up the wages of the company's remaining workers.[†] Only those companies with a competitive advantage in the marketplace can survive such tactical manipulation. One of the most well-known public (and legal) cartels is the Organization of Petroleum Exporting Countries (OPEC). The organization consists of twelve oil exporting countries in the Middle East that determine the policies of exporting oil.[†] Their operation also controls and determines the price of it, thereby directly manipulating the cycle of supply and demand. This controversial organization has people all over the world up in arms over OPEC's practice of walking the thin line between operating a legitimate business and an outright monopoly. It can be argued labor unions behave similarly because many of their strong-armed tactics that force companies to comply with providing higher wages increase price points on their product or service to the consumer. If a company is forced to increase wages, it will likely pass that cost onto the consumer.

Taxing a Company's Bottom Line

Samuel Gompers, one of the fathers of the union movement once said, "The worst crime against working people is a company which fails to operate at a profit." If he only knew how today's unions are hurting America's businesses, I think he would be ashamed.

For America's businesses, staying competitive in today's global marketplace is nearly impossible. Many companies who have allowed union organization to occur and, as we will examine in this chapter, have gone out of business as a result of unionizing. For the few companies fortunate enough to survive unionization, it is likely they are doing so by dipping into their profits. And when companies dig too deeply into those coveted and sometimes razor-thin profit margins, they are forced to forgo things like research and development (R&D) and capital investments.

Take General Motors, for example. We all know how the economic downturn has devastated America's auto industry. Consider this scenario: In November 2008, the United States auto industry was reeling after posting the worst monthly U.S. sales results in the past 25 years. GM led the downfall with a drop of 45 percent, followed by Chrysler posting a decline of 35 percent and Ford at a 30.2 percent loss. Mike DiGiovanni, GM's chief sales analyst said October's annual selling rate was the lowest since 1982, a year when the economy experienced its worst recession since the Depression.[†] Analysts speculated GM may delay its plans for research and development of its new car, the Chevrolet Cruze, a fuel-efficient compact car slated to launch in 2010, something many thought would be a mistake. "Any of the Detroit Three that are having to consider pulling back on R&D spending are missing the opportunity to beat the Japanese automakers at what I think is the weakest element of what they offer, and that is design." This was stated by Phil Biggs, an automotive leader at Crowne Horwath LLC in Grand Rapids[†]

Obviously, the drastic decrease in sales is not solely a result of union influence garnering large pensions and benefits. The economy was in turmoil during this time and Americans simply were not buying cars. But the fact these automakers were experiencing such desperation to begin with, can be traced back to unions forcing automakers into paying benefits and pensions they simply could not afford.

Economists and academics have studied unions and their influence for years with many of them demonstrating their negative impact on America's businesses and our economy at large. A study conducted by Barry T. Hirsch, an economist with Florida State University and researcher of unions, reviewed the impact unions had on U.S. companies and their profitability and market value in the 1970s, when union membership began a steady decline. Hirsch analyzed 705 publicly-traded U.S. companies finding that unionized companies earn profits approximately 20 percent lower than those of comparable non-union firms.[†]

Author and consultant Peter J. Bergeron wrote a book about how to keep your company out of the hands of unions titled *Union Proof – Creating Your Successful Union Free Strategy*. In it, he discussed the tremendous financial impact unions have on a company. According to Bergeron, the cost of running a unionized company is estimated to be 25-35 percent higher than a union-free organization. This is due to the expense of garnering more human resource staff, boosting legal counsel, and dealing with increased labor costs due to rules on overtime, grievances and time lost while in negotiations.[†]

Projections, Inc. is a company providing union-free communications resources and solutions to companies. In an article posted on their website titled, "The Cost of Unionization, Projections, Inc." referenced Jim Gray, president of Jim Gray Consultants. A similar consulting firm found that businesses could expect to spend approximately $400,000 to more than $2,000,000 in a single unionization campaign. In fact, according to Gray, additional annual operating expenses for a unionized firm could range from $900,000 for a company with 100 employees, to more than $4,000,000 for companies with 2,000 employees or more. In his estimates, these operating expenses do not include benefits or wages but items such as training for managers, additional Human Resource support, attorney and consultant fees, strike planning and lost productivity...hiking expenses even more.[†] Competitive companies, in this day in age, simply cannot foot the bill for such large increases to their budgets without collapsing or passing the costs along to the consumer.

Unions: Unified Voice for Whom?

Unions claim to speak with a unified voice for their members. While that may be true, it has caused workers to lose their individuality and desire to succeed or perform well on the job. Unions also preach that their members earn more money in wages and benefits than their non-union counterparts. A study conducted by the Bureau of Labor Statistics in September 2009, supports these claims by stating non-union employers paid an average of $19.06 per hour in wages while unionized employers in the same sector were required to pay $22.76 per hour. Benefits calculated similarly with non-union members earning $7.33 per hour in benefits while unionized employees earned $13.82 in benefits.

Union-Negotiated Pensions Fail to
Compare to Non-Unionized Plans

Unions recruit new members under the guise of promising those higher wages and generous pension benefits. What these workers don't know is these pension promises are actually smaller and less significant than non-union negotiated pension packages.

In the Fall of 2009, the U.S. Labor Department issued a study showing many of the collectively bargained pension funds were under-funded compared to other pension programs, putting union members at a disadvantage. In 2006, the most recent year for which full statistical data was available, only 17 percent of union-negotiated plans were fully funded. This compares with 35 percent of non-union plans.

As defined by the Pension Protection Act of 2006, a whopping 41 percent of union funds were considered "endangered" while only 14 percent of non-union funds fit in that category.[†] Diana Furchtgott-Roth, a senior fellow and director of the Hudson Institute's Center for Employment Policy and former chief economist at the U.S. Labor Department credits this to a variety of faults by unions. Furchtgott-Roth told the Washington Examiner, "One possible reason for the disparity is that collectively-bargained pension plans are not usually renewed annually," she said. "As a result, annual contributions by employers may not respond quickly to market downturns or other unexpected drops in pension funding ratios. Furthermore, when a union must negotiate with several different employers, this problem is exacerbated."

Unions typically prefer to use a "template" type plan where the amount is pre-determined and guaranteed in advance of the worker's retirement. This amount is usually calculated by averaging the worker's highest paid three to five years on the job and then guaranteeing a percentage of that amount. The catch? These workers must stay in unionized jobs in order to reap full benefit of these plans.

On the flip side, non-unionized firms typically offer 401(k) where the employee can choose to contribute part of their salary and the employer may match it. Workers are entitled to legally "claim" the money and can take it with them when they leave the job without being penalized.

Furchtgott-Roth says flexibility is one reason unions cringe at defined contribution plans. "They enable workers to leave a union job for a non-union job where they frequently get higher pay and bonuses," she said. "With the collectively bargained plans, you might have to stay for a long time before getting any benefits and there are big penalties for leaving early. This prevents workers from being upwardly mobile."

Unions might also scoff at these contribution plans because they don't always offer instant gratification to the worker such as higher wages. "Union leaders are more concerned with trumpeting what they can get in the paycheck now, instead of what they can get in the future," Furchtgott-Roth said. "There's no incentive for delayed economic gratification, that's what we call a high discount rate. Leaning on employers to ensure the pension is well-funded takes much work for little visible effect."[†]

To summarize, pension plans negotiated for members by unions don't stack up to non-unionized plans. Sounds outrageous, right? It gets worse.

According to Furchtgott-Roth, pension benefits for officers and staffers of unions themselves faired far better than the ones they negotiated for their members. A sample of 30 union staff pension plans revealed that while collectively bargained plans (negotiated by unions) had 70 percent of the funds needed to satisfy their obligations, union officers' own plans were 93 percent funded. Furchtgott-Roth surmised that the high-level of coverage shows unions know how to fund a pension plan properly, "if they choose to." There should be no reason why unions can't get better plans negotiated for their members when their own officers have excellent ones.

Stifling Hard Work, One Worker at a Time

Innovation and the incentive to perform well on the job are squashed by unions. Consider the young factory worker who earns a smaller salary than the worker standing next to him on the assembly line doing the exact same job. His co-worker is paid a higher salary merely because of his seniority not because he is more skilled or has more experience. Unions typically create contracts based on pre-determined job categories and base pay and promotions on seniority.

Based on findings resulting from a study conducted by Richard B. Freeman, it has been found that unions' wage structure, within establishments, creates an environment that routinely negotiates pay based on job classifications and seniority rather than individual job performance or ability.[†]

What sort of incentive do you think the younger worker has to do a good job for a company that does not recognize his achievement in the workplace if the only way to get a raise is by punching the clock more times? Unions destroy and stifle innovation and the need to better or improve performance. How can we, as Americans, remain competitive in an intense global market when we no longer reward workers for a job well done? Some of our country's greatest inventions and financial successes were accomplished due to our desire to achieve current and future financial stability.

Unions Cause Job Losses

A study conducted by Freeman and Kleiner found that unionized firms shed jobs more frequently and expand less frequently than non-union firms. Unionized companies who are forced to pay their workers more often, need to lay off a percentage of their workforce to do so, and find themselves in an unstable position if a hiring need arises.

Unionization can also lead to outsourcing – a business element the Democratic Party seems to vehemently oppose and yet their union friends are causing this shift to occur. Consider this: if a customer support division of a technology company employed 30 unionized workers but found they could outsource their customer service support at half the cost, it's obvious they would chose outsourcing. Among a deteriorating workforce and rising unemployment numbers, this situation could lead to other countries having a competitive advantage in labor.

A study conducted by Francis Kramarz in 2006 analyzed French labor tendencies and outsourcing statistics. He found that outsourcing of labor to countries such as Africa, Latin America and Asia has been partially driven by unions. Not surprisingly, the companies studied found it more cost-efficient to outsource their labor than to bend to the insurmountable costs unions thrust upon them.[†]

Calculating data researched by economists Barry T. Hirsch and David Macpherson, the Heritage Foundation found information dispelling the common misperception that manufacturing jobs have been disappearing over the last 30 years. This is not necessarily the case. While manufacturing jobs have fallen in both the union and non-union sectors since 2000, their analysis shows that between 1977 and 2008, unionized manufacturing jobs fell by 75 percent while non-union manufacturing jobs actually increased by six percent during that same time period.[†]

Unions Discourage Investors

Investors typically view unionization as reducing the company's market value.

Research has shown unionization can reduce a company's cumulative return to investors by ten percent over two years.[†]

Unions' effect on the stock market and a company's ability to invest in itself after organizing, has been studied by multiple economists over the years. Much of this research has found that unionized companies tend to invest less in physical capital and research and development than non-unionized companies do. One study, conducted by Barry T. Hirsch, found that while union investment effects vary among industries, "unionized companies invest roughly 20 percent less in physical capital than do similar non-union companies." He found that about half of this percentage appears to be a direct union effect, where a union's tax on future earnings from capital stock, while the other half accounts for an indirect impact from unions resulting from lower current earnings among unionized companies.[†]

The bottom line is, less investment hampers a company's ability to compete, which in turn, endangers jobs *and* wages.

Unions Prolong Economic Recovery

By demanding higher pay for workers, businesses must dip into their profits to cover the cost, often resulting in decreased profitability, cutting jobs, limiting innovation and advancement through research and development. The results are devastating to businesses trying to survive in a competitive market, as-well-as devastating to the general economy. As expected, this is particularly harmful during a recession. Studies show that during the 1982 and 1991 recessions, states with a greater number of union members took considerably longer to recover from a recession than states that had lower membership volume. This is a topic we will delve into further when we discuss the tremendous benefits of right to work protection laws.

The book, *Out of Work: Unemployment and Government in Twentieth-Century America* also examines the impact of unions on unemployment. The findings are similar in that unions can have a negative impact on employment rates across time – not just following recessions. Analyzing regional data, Professors Vedder and Gallaway found unemployment numbers were lower in states that had "relatively high agricultural employment, modest levels of unionization and a comparatively modest incidence of public assistance."[†]

In September, 2009, touting the need for healthcare reform, President Barack Obama spoke before a group of autoworkers near a General Motors plant near Youngstown, Ohio. He was reaching out to a voter base that played a big role in electing him president, trying to get them on board with his reform plan. In addition to healthcare,

President Obama discussed the economy and took credit for its improvement over the past several months – thanks to his policies. He told the autoworkers the government had little choice but to intervene, to prevent a collapse of the American auto industry, and because of this intervention their company had restructured themselves and was heading back from collapse. He told them, "Your survival and the success of our economy depend on making sure that we get the U.S. auto industry back on its feet." He told them the Cash for Clunkers program, which offered drivers up to $4,500 to buy more fuel-efficient cars, was a big contributor to the turn-around of their company. With the clunkers program, GM's Chevrolet Cobalt was one of the most sought-after cars. As a result, GM increased production of the car and rehired laid-off workers.

President Obama told them, "Because of the steps we've taken, this plant is about to shift into high gear A hundred and fifty of your co-workers came back to work yesterday. More than a thousand will be coming back to work in less than three weeks as the production of the Cobalt ramps up."[†]

While it may be true that the Cash for Clunkers stimulated car buying and boosted auto sales for America's automakers, the fact remains it was a temporary fix – a Band-Aid on a wound that simply will not heal without some serious retooling within the auto industry. Consider this: Nearly 700,000 people took advantage of the Cash for Clunkers program and probably got a good deal on a new car. The thousands of shoppers that bought cars during August, 2009 and shortly thereafter likely overpaid. Prices for cars during the Clunkers program went up across the board – for everyone. People who were able to use the program saved about $3,000 versus those that did not. Cash for Clunkers ended August 24th and for the next few months, people buying vehicles likely paid more to buy the exact same car. Why? Supply and demand – the Cash for Clunkers program threw the system off because inventory was lower than planned, and to compensate, car lots raised prices and offered fewer selections on vehicles.[†]

While President Obama and Transportation Secretary Ray LaHood can pat themselves on the back for a stimulus program, they shouldn't be popping the corks on the champagne. Cash for Clunkers was a quick fix for an ailing auto industry. Sure, it stimulated car buying and factories rehired workers but how long that honeymoon will last is the big question. Chances are, not long. Within months of restocking their inventory, showrooms will likely be full again and automakers will once again shrug their shoulders, wondering why they are still in the red. Unless they take action like drastically scaling back on union agendas and influence, automakers will be stuck chasing Toyota and other foreign automakers much like rabbits after the coveted carrot. Aligning wages and benefits with industry standards will free up funds for GM to finance research and development – something they've lacked for years. Then, when they create a car Americans want to buy, sales will go up, profits will expand and jobs will be protected. Then, and only then will a permanent solution help the auto industry.

Other policies that mask themselves as helping the American worker are the New Deal policies from the 1930's and National Labor Relations Act or the "Wagner Act". Interestingly, studies have actually found these monumental pieces of legislation *delay* recovery. In fact, when President Franklin Roosevelt signed the Act in 1935, it prolonged and actually deepened the Great Depression. This, coupled with the fact he permitted industries to reduce output and raise prices (a cartel-like behavior) and only if companies in that industry unionized and paid above-market wages. Companies were paying above-average wages in an economy struggling to stabilize. Labor and industry policies associated with the New Deal did not lift the country out of depression as President Roosevelt had hoped. Instead, it taxed businesses by increasing labor's bargaining influence and forced companies to pay wages that were too high for them to support. This caused half of the economic losses that occurred in the 1930s.[†]

Mirroring some of the New Deal policies set forth by President Roosevelt in the 1930s, it appears the Obama administration is headed in the same direction-touting initiatives that will likely prolong an already painful recession. The Employee Free Choice Act, which, at the time of this writing was stalled in Congress, is a piece of legislation that would eliminate secret ballots for organizing unions and strip business owners of the decision-making ability to negotiate contracts. It would essentially put government bureaucrats in charge of running our nation's businesses, reversing the American Dream and killing American jobs.

† See appendix for reference.

"The proper business of a labor union is to get higher wages, better hours and good shop conditions for the workmen. But when labor en masse plunks its vote for its own party, then the spirit of party loyalty begins to obscure labor's objectives – high wages, short hours, decent shop conditions. Thus class-conscious labor leaders become more interested in their party welfare than in the fundamental objectives of the labor unions. So we shall have the class-conscious political worker trading his vote not for the immediate objective of wages, hours and shop conditions, but for power for his political labor boss."
– William Allen White
Speech, Sep. 20, 1937

CHAPTER FIVE

The Strong-Arm of a Union

The Influence of Union Agendas on Politics

Historically, unions have had a strong grip on Washington. In fact, unions played a tremendous role in electing President Obama. According to the Center for Responsive Politics, labor unions reportedly spent a whopping $43.5 million on communications and independent expenditures for President Obama's presidential campaign and $6.6 million to defeat his Republican opponent, Senator John McCain. Employees of unions spent more than $470,000 in direct donations to President Obama's campaign compared to contributions to Senator John McCain's campaign which totaled $25,000.[†]

One is left wondering if such financial influence may sway a politician. In his book, *The Audacity of Hope*, Obama wrote, "I owe those unions. When their leaders call, I do my best to call them right away. I don't consider this corrupting in any way; I don't mind feeling obligated..."[†] I don't know about you, but I am uncomfortable having the leader of one of the largest nations in the world feeling "obligated" to return a phone call to a union leader.

Of course, President Obama isn't the only one who has benefited enormously from the unions and their members' hard-earned dues that are inevitably used to finance these campaigns. Most recently, in the 2008 election, unions elected more members to Congress than any other time in recent history and spent big bucks doing it. According to the Center for Responsive Politics, unions reportedly spent $80 million on independent broadcast advertising, mail and internal advocacy to help elect or defeat certain federal candidates. The Service Employees International Union alone reportedly spent a mind-blowing $42.4 million in the 2008 elections. These independent expenditures were on top of the more than $73 million the labor sector contributed directly to candidates' campaigns and to party committees. This is a 20% increase over what was spent in the 2004 elections.[†]

Unions' strategy worked. The top ten candidates unions spent the most money to defeat, lost their elections. Of the top ten candidates labor spent money on supporting, only one lost – Louisiana's Donald Cazayoux.[†]

Union political influence can go even deeper. Before being appointed to the United States Labor Secretary post, U.S. Representative Hilda Solis was a candidate who reaped the benefits of organized labor's financial donations to her campaigns. As a former board member for the American Rights at Work organization (a pro-union organization that advocates for the Employee Free Choice Act) it's easy to see why Solis would collect campaign contributions from union interests – and it is astonishing to see exactly how much she collected. According to the Center for Responsive Politics, during her time at the House of Representatives and since 1999, Solis received $888,050 from the labor sector. In fact, 15 of her top 20 contributors were labor unions such as the United Auto Workers and Carpenters & Joiners Union.[†]

As one might imagine, Solis' appointment to the Labor Secretary post caused quite a stir among Washington's Republican leaders. Not only was she the only member of Congress to serve on the American Rights at Work Board of Directors in 2007, she co-sponsored the Employee Free Choice Act, a highly controversial bill that would make it easier for unions to organize. In her initial appointment hearing before the Senate Committee on Health, Education, Labor & Pensions,

Solis faced serious questioning, including a formal questionnaire and allegations that her four year tenure with the American Rights at Work organization created a conflict of interest. American Rights at Work is documented as having lobbied Congress on passage of the Employee Free Choice Act. In disclosure forms filed with the White House prior to her appointment, Solis reportedly omitted her board work with the American Rights at Work. Later she sent a letter to the House clerk on January 29th correcting the documents, saying she was a board member and the treasurer.

Republican Senators, namely Senator Michael Enzi, questioned whether Solis' involvement with the organization created an ethical dilemma and suggested the situation would clash with President Obama's new ethics policy. The ethics policy states that appointees who lobbied on an issue must steer clear of it for a period of two years before government service. The questionnaire asked Solis if she intended to seek a waiver from the Obama administration or avoid any role in passing the legislation once it arrived in Congress. Solis insisted she did not need a waiver and had no intention of stepping back from the bill. She insisted she was only a member of Congress exercising her powers and was not paid for her work with the organization. She said, "I am not a registered lobbyist, nor do I in any way meet the statutory requirements for registration of a lobbyist."[†]

Republicans also questioned whether Solis violated a House of Representatives rule that bans members from lobbying practices, on behalf of a private organization, even if that work is done for free. At this point, Solis deferred all questions to the White House who issued the statement: "Representative Solis was not involved in any way in personally supervising any lobbying activities by American Rights at Work and her services as a board member and treasurer of the organization in no way conflicted with her obligations as a member."[†]

Senate Republicans, while still concerned about Solis' record, decided not to subject her nomination to a filibuster and confirmed her nomination on February 24, 2009.[†]

What does all this political financing mean? Among other things, it means unions are getting louder in the political arena – using their member's dues to speak for all union workers. The ethical line is getting harder and harder to distinguish. Interestingly, many of its own members – the supposed Unified Voice – are left feeling disgruntled with the allocation of their hard earned dues, leaving unions facing the worst public opinion in its history.

† See appendix for reference.

"A house divided among itself cannot stand."
                                    – Abraham Lincoln

CHAPTER SIX

A House Divided

The Future of Unions

U nions saw a small increase in membership in 2008, reversing
years of decline. Still, only about 12.4 percent of American
workers belong to unions, including 7.6 percent of private industry
employees – about half of what it was 25 years ago.[†] The decline in
interest and relevance can be attributed to a number of factors, many
of which we've already covered. Unions have done an excellent job
securing important labor laws that prohibit poor working conditions
and regulate work hours. Without legislation like the Fair Labor
Standards Act, our country would not be as healthy as it is today,
recessional bumps and all. But even in the face of the worst economic
crisis our country has seen in decades, unions can do little for today's
workers. In fact, some analysis shows union influence has been known
to *decrease* a worker's wages.

In an increasingly competitive global marketplace, more and more
companies simply cannot give into demands like wage and benefit
increases. Unions, using their bargaining power, would take it from
someone else. It is a classic "rob Peter to pay Paul" scenario, except in
this case, everyone loses. They would go out of business and not only
would workers not get an increase in wages, they would be out of a
job.

One study analyzed changes in manufacturing companies before and after successful unionization elections. The study found after unionization, employment among production employees actually dropped 11 percent within two years of the election and wages did not rise (as was most likely promised). As common sense would dictate, the same study also found productivity to fall as well.[†]

I recently came across a news article about a union/city hall dispute in Allentown, Pennsylvania. The local Service Employees International Union informed the Allentown City Council of its intentions to file a grievance against the city because a member of the community was infringing on their employment opportunities. The complaint was based on a volunteer clearing a walking path in a nearby park. The culprit? A boy scout. That's right. The union had a big issue with an Eagle Scout candidate who, in the pursuit of earning his badge, had logged more than 200 hours working to clear a better walking and biking trail in the park. The union was likely reacting to a decision the city made months earlier to lay off 39 SEIU members. Nick Balzano, president of the SEIU said, "There are to be no volunteers." Basically, if his union members couldn't be hired to work on a project *no one* should be – not even volunteers.

Mayor Ed Pawlowski told the local newspaper, "We would hope that the well-intentioned efforts of an Eagle Scout candidate would not be challenged by the unions. This young man is performing a great service to the community. His efforts should be recognized as such."

Perhaps responding to an outcry by local residents, Balzano backed off his stance and said, "We are probably going to let this one go." The audacity of unions going after an innocent boy scout boggles my mind and clearly exemplifies unions' self-serving mentality.

President Abraham Lincoln once said of the United States at odds, "A house divided among itself cannot stand." The same can be said for today's unions. Infighting among leadership within unions themselves indicates trouble. In 2005 six unions, including heavy hitters such as the Service Employees, Teamsters and the United Food and

Commercial Workers, broke from the AFL-CIO citing they weren't aggressive enough in organizing new companies. Together, they formed the "Change to Win" coalition. Reports of conflict, regime changes and finger pointing among the biggest unions have continued making storylines.

With unemployment numbers projected to climb beyond 10% amid a dismal recession, one might think our economic crisis would have boosted confidence and membership in America's unions, but the opposite appears to have occurred. A Gallup poll conducted in August, 2009 found the public's support of unions has hit the lowest point in history, since Gallup began asking the question in 1936. Forty-eight percent of those polled approved of a union, which is down from the 59 percent approval rating from the same time the year before. Similarly, disapproval jumped to 45 percent from 31 percent in the same period. Until 2009, the public's approval ratings have always been above 50 percent. For additional perspective, when the question was first asked in 1936, 72 percent of respondents approved of unions and even as recently as 2003, approval ratings hovered around the 65 percent mark. A disconnect and distrust seems to be growing among the American public as we learn more and more about the weight unions have on our economy. The same poll found 66 percent believe unions help workers who are union members, but 62 percent believe unions "mostly hurt" non-union workers who make up approximately 88 percent of the workforce. A surprising 51 percent said unions "mostly hurt" the economy in general.[†]

It is clear the American people are growing outraged as the perception of bloated benefits and pension packages, given to unionized state and local government workers, are unfair – at the taxpayer expense. This sentiment comes at a time when most private-sector workers are facing job furloughs, pay cuts and reductions to their 401K plans.

Recently, in my home state of Arizona, members of the local UFCW union threatened to enlist their 25,000 members to strike if two major grocery stores; Fry's Food and Drug, and Safeway, didn't comply with their demands. The big bone of contention was the stores' proposal that employees, who were not paying anything for health insurance, be required to pay some of the cost. The stores pointed out the economy had negatively impacted their profits, and in order to stay afloat, it's employees needed to pick up a little slack. The gigantic amount that made the unions balk? Between $5 per week for single health coverage to $15 for family health coverage. That's it. I guarantee most insurance-paying families in American are paying more than that to support their health coverage. Not to mention, paying a little more out-of-pocket for health care is a whole heck of a lot better than not getting any at all…when the grocery store goes bankrupt.

As the clocked ticked onward and negotiations appeared to have stalled, employees began getting nervous about the impending strike. Both stores had been placing help wanted ads in the newspapers and out-of-work Arizonans lined up for the chance at employment.

Many union members began speaking out against the unions and even held a rally protesting the impending strike. Sean Owen, a union member told the *Arizona Republic*, "I don't want to go on strike. Not in this economy." Another employee, Kim Cress, echoed his sentiments, "I can't believe the union is calling for a strike in this economy." Cress, an 18-year union member quit the union the day before. Fry's employee Maria Vavra told the *Republic* she was worried about her job.

Does this sound like an organization, a unified voice, who is concerned for its members? I don't think so.

Even more challenging for the unions, the public ill-will and disapproval of unions comes at a crossroads, as the AFL-CIO lobbies Congress for the Employee Free Choice Act, which would make it easier for workers to organize. Have they waited too long? Is it too late for unions to strong-arm their way into more legislation and push more regulations onto America's businesses?

† See appendix for reference.

"One of the cornerstones of any democracy is the right of its citizens to make fully informed political choices by voting in elections: in private, free from fear of retaliation, coercion, ridicule or pressure of any type, peer or otherwise."

– U.S. Chamber of Commerce
EFCA BOOK

CHAPTER SEVEN

Employee Free Choice Act

Coerscion and Limiting Freedom

The so-called Employee Free Choice Act (EFCA) is a labor bill currently floating around Congress and has been a lighting rod of controversy. If passed, it would arguably be one of the most sweeping reforms President Barack Obama would undertake in office to date. The Act, also known as "Card Check," would eliminate secret ballot voting among workers looking to unionize. It would replace the secret ballot, organizing instead, elections with publicly signed union cards— leaving the door open for union leaders to harass and bully workers into signing union cards. Presently, a worker can vote "no" behind a curtain or with secret ballots, but would be likely to feel less inclined to do so in public.[†]

Supporters of the legislation claim the Act will increase union membership thereby bolstering wages and improving social welfare, overall.[†] It's true, union membership will likely increase – when workers feel undue pressure to organize.

EFCA also creates government-run workplaces by imposing drastic limitations on newly organized businesses. This gives government bureaucrats, who likely have little, if any experience in industry, power to dictate how a business is run. Card check legislation would allow government to impose collective bargaining rules and contract regulations such as pre-determined wages, benefits, employment rankings, business operations, promotions, assignments and merging. (HR 1409) This sweeping, drastic legislation would potentially affect up to four million small businesses that employ 39 million Americans.[†]

It isn't hard to see why unions are lobbying so hard for this legislation. According to a Workforce Fairness Institute report, passage of the EFCA would be extremely profitable for union bosses – to the tune of $35 billion over the next ten years in dues paid to unions.[†] With even more money lining their pockets, unions would have even *more* funding to spend on political elections, giving them even *more* power and clout, essentially destroying our country's agenda and direction.

Not all unions support EFCA. Keith Smith, director of employment and labor policy at the National Association of Manufacturers, is among the many who oppose the EFCA. "This opens the door to government wage controls," he said. "That means that someone who's unfamiliar with the company could set the terms of wages, benefits and work rules. It's really a hindrance to our ability to create and retain jobs." The National Association of Manufacturers is one of the groups leading the opposition to this bill and has spent $13.7 million on lobbying in the last two years. "This is a clear de-stimulus if there ever was one," Smith said. "It's hard to justify EFCA at any time, but especially a time like now."[†]

Chris Hudgins, vice president of government relations and policy at the International Sleep Products Association agrees. "We think there's a fair process in place. Obviously, a great institution in this country has been the secret ballot, and we're very worried about taking that away," he said. "It really puts everything out in the open and allows the system to be corrupted."[†]

Research demonstrates that passage of the EFCA would drastically alter labor relations and would ultimately change the landscape of the U.S. economy. By increasing union membership, we are forcing businesses to increase wages and benefits – compelling them to offset the costs elsewhere which will likely result in the loss of jobs, impacting the nation's unemployment rate. On a broader level, increasing union membership and wages will have a chilling effect on the economy as companies find it necessary to pass the cost on to consumers to cover higher wages. Higher wages and a decreased workforce is a bad idea in a tumultuous economy. The effects of EFCA, as unintentional as they may be, will be disastrous for our country.

On the most basic level, passage of the EFCA would inevitably cause unemployment to rise. Conservative estimates calculated by the Heritage Foundation show that EFCA would reduce employment opportunities by 765,000 potential jobs over the next seven years.[†]

Investments would also suffer with the passage of EFCA. In 2009, a study conducted by David S. Lee, a professor of economics at Princeton University and Alexandre Mas, an associate professor at the University of California Berkeley, analyzed the impact unions have on investors. By using event-study methodologies analyzing data, they tracked how the stock market reacted to union victories (up to 48 months before and after a union election) in various publicly traded companies. Part of their analysis included looking at companies whose workers voted narrowly in favor of organizing and companies whose workers voted narrowly against organizing. They found about a ten percent decline, or about $40,500 per unionized worker over two years. Lee and Mas calculated that passage of the Employee Free Choice Act would result in reducing the average market value of all companies by about 4.3 percent.[†]

Business owners and investors aren't the only ones opposing the Act. The Coalition for a Democratic Workplace, a pro-union organization known for worker advocacy, recently financed a poll that found 74% of union members favor keeping the current system. Other findings illustrated union members' concern over the threat of secret ballots, worker privacy and job growth.

Brian Worth, spokesman for the Coalition for a Democratic Workplace said, "The strong opposition from current union members to the Employee Free Choice Act should send a clear signal to

President Obama and the Democrat-controlled Congress. The EFCA lacks popular support, both among key Democratic constituency and voters as a whole. The only support card check has is among the leaders of Big Labor."[†]

More and more Democrats are dropping their support of the bill as well. EFCA lost a lot of steam when Senator Arlen Specter and others backed away from supporting it. Even U.S. Representative Todd Platts, a former Teamster who "appreciates the importance of unions," calls the bill a "job killer."[†]

Not only is EFCA bad for the economy, its' premise is very un-American. Imposing a pressure-cooker situation on a worker is the very issue our forefathers fought to destroy. EFCA is a disservice to our country and the middle class – the very group unions say they want to protect. Through EFCA, unions are once again finding ways to kill American jobs.

† See appendix for reference.

"What you've created here is better than communism, better than socialism could even be, better even than capitalism. I like to call what you've got here "enlightened consumerism," where everybody works together as a team and the customer is finally king again."

> *– Paul Harvey*
> *radio commentator*
> *commenting on Wal-Mart*
> *(Walton, Sam).*

CHAPTER EIGHT

A Success Story

Building a Profitable Business
Without Unions

It is clear unions have had a tremendous impact on both our country's successes and failures. Some of our nations' strongest and most successful companies have taken a very strong stand against unions. Companies and organizations such as FedEx, the Associated Builders and Contractors and even the United States Chamber of Commerce all oppose unionization. Of course, analyzing unions and their impact on our country would not be complete without taking a brief look at a company that has staved off union advances for decades and is arguably, one of the most successful companies in the entire world.

Love 'em or hate 'em, Wal-Mart's success speaks for itself. Through their 55 various banners, the discount retailer serves customers more than 200 million times per week at more than 8,000 retail stores in 15 countries. In Fiscal Year 2009, Wal-Mart's sales topped $401 billion[†] in addition to being ranked first among general merchandisers in Fortune Magazine's 2009 Most Admired Companies survey.[†] However you feel about the mega-discounter, it's hard to ignore the tremendous success it has experienced over the past several decades. In the United States, Wal-Mart is the largest private employer with an estimated 1.4 million employees covering over 4,300 stores.[†] Sam Walton, founder of Wal-Mart, had a brilliant business plan and philosophy when it came to treatment of their employees and their policy against unionizing.

It could be said the landscape of American retail was changed with the opening of the first Wal-Mart store in 1962, in Rogers, Arkansas. Walton believed in offering the lowest price for the best possible product and took pride in providing his customers with exemplary customer service. After incorporating and then going public, Walton worked to pour investor capital into the company and it grew to 276 stores in 11 states by the end of 1979. In 1983, Walton opened the first membership warehouse, Sam's Club, and in 1988 opened the first Wal-Mart Supercenter. Wal-Mart became an international company in 1991 with its first Sam's Club near Mexico City, Mexico and has expanded steadily since.

Sam Walton believed the key to Wal-Mart's success was not in the merchandising or distribution – it was in how he treated his associates. "Our relationship with the associates is a partnership in the truest sense," he said. "It's the only reason our company has been able to consistently outperform the competition – and even our own expectations."

"Associates." You don't hear that term every day when referring to the folks who work for you at a grocery store. Walton's insistence on calling every employee an "associate" illustrated his intent on creating an "all for one, one for all" teamwork atmosphere. Walton believed that by giving his associates a stake in the company, they would take pride in their work and perform better on the job, ultimately contributing to the company's success. Walton wrote in his autobiography, "The more you share profits with your associates – whether it's in salaries or incentives or bonuses or stock discounts – the more profit will accrue to the company. Why? Because the way management treats the associates is exactly how the associates will then treat the customers. And if the associates treat the customers well, the customers will return again and again and *that* is where the real profit in this business lies…"

In addition to offering competitive wages and health care benefits, full-time Wal-Mart associates enjoy benefits that include profit sharing, incentive bonuses and discount stock purchase plans. Management also makes an effort to involve associates in business planning and instills a solid foundation of open communications with all associates.

Wal-Mart's "Open Door" policy further demonstrates the commitment to a team culture. Wal-Mart states this policy means associates are free to share suggestions, ideas and voice concerns; whether it's help with a problem, guidance or directions, or simply getting an answer to a question.

Treating associates like business partners exemplifies corporate synergy and eliminates any need for union involvement. In his autobiography, *Made in America*, Walton writes:

> *"I have always believed strongly that we don't need unions at Wal-Mart. Theoretically, I understand the argument that unions try to make, that the associates need someone to represent them and so on. But historically, as unions have developed in this country, they have mostly just been divisive. They have put management on one side of the fence, employees on the other, and themselves in the middle as almost a separate business, one that depends on division between the other camps. And divisiveness, by breaking down direct communication, makes it harder to take care of customers, to be competitive, and to gain market share."*

Simply put, unions would lead to higher operating costs and less flexibility in managing workers. Walton recalls his labor attorney, John Tate telling him, "Take care of your people, treat them well, involve them and you won't spend your time and money hiring labor lawyers to fight unions."[†]

If only it were that easy. Over the years Wal-Mart has spent millions of dollars and resources trying to thwart union influence and for the most part, they've been quite successful. According to Wal-Mart, the United Food and Commercial Workers have tried multiple times over the years to unionize Wal-Mart associates – usually by concentrating on a particular segment like the Tire and Lube Express unit or the Meat Cutters. Rather than face defeat, in multiple instances, unions have blocked or canceled elections. In a press release acknowledging the union's cancellation of an election, Jay Allen, vice president of corporate affairs stated, "It's a shame the UFCW chooses to tie up these processes rather than acknowledge they've lost support. The UFCW says they are trying to give associates a voice in the workplace, yet they are the ones continuing to silence them."[†] Mary Chapman, an associate at a Sam's Club in Las Vegas, Nevada chalks up the cancellation of an election at her store as cowardly. "The UFCA organizers are afraid to let us vote because they know they would lose," she said. "Why do you think they blocked our election in the first place? They are like vultures. They keep circling and circling even though we had 140 associates send them letters asking them to bow out and leave us alone."[†]

Trying to pick up steam for the EFCA however, Wal-Mart says the UFCW has intensified its efforts in attempting to organize its associates. In an article for the *Washington Post*, David Tovar, a company spokesman said, "We have noticed that the UFCW has been working harder lately in its attempts to get Wal-Mart associates to sign union cards, but we don't think our associates have any reason to be more interested than before." This same article stated that in early Spring of 2009, about 60 UFCW organizers have been dispatched to more than 100 Wal-Mart stores in 15 states to get workers to sign union-authorization cards.[†]

As I've stated, labor unions have made an incredible impact on our country's workforce and economy and should be credited with improving the landscape for America's workers. Great strides have been made in improving working conditions, assuring workers are compensated fairly and have a safe work environment. In fact, some of our nation's greatest worker-protection laws have been put into place by unions. But as labor laws and our global economy have evolved our need for union representation has been eliminated. We should all take note of Sam Walton's policy on union representation in the workplace and work to discourage harmful union orgaization. NOT to *stifle* the voices of our workers or associates, but to *encourage* open communication between management and workers. The result will be a more synergistic business model with increased profitability, a happier staff and fewer headaches. Allowing our nation's businesses the right to work is key to economic success and sustainability.

Today's unions only serve to discourage profitability. Instead of offering workers a voice, unions have largely become a third wheel, a nasty *wedge* between employer and employee. This *wedge* is disrupting and destroying our economy, our businesses and our workers – the very people unions say they want to protect.

"The prudent, penniless beginner in the world, labors for wages awhile, saves a surplus with which to buy tools or land, for himself; the labors on his own account another while, and a length hires another new beginner to help him. This...is free labor — the just and generous system, which opens the way for all."

– Abraham Lincoln

The Job Builder

Synergy in the Workplace

It was a moment relived time and again, in highlighted reels, as one of the greatest Super Bowl moments in history - the stuff legends are made of. It was January 22, 1989 – Super Bowl XXIII – the San Francisco 49ers were trailing the Cincinnati Bengals by three points. The air inside Joe Robbie Stadium was thick with anticipation as quarterback Joe Montana and his teammates returned to the field after a timeout. After a quick snap, Montana spotted Jerry Rice in the end zone and rocket-fired the ball right into Rice's hands, winning the game with seconds remaining.[†] The play was flawless and appeared effortless in its execution. While an outsider could chalk up the play to athletic skill, it took both players working together to achieve magic. Joe Montana and Jerry Rice displayed awe-inspiring synergy – the perfect blend of skill and talent to achieve greatness. Independently, they were both phenomenal players. Montana is arguably one of the best quarterbacks ever to play the game. Rice also shares a long and storied career, regarded as one of the most successful wide receivers in the NFL. Separately, they were phenomenal but together they found kismet, igniting each other, complimenting each other's specific skill sets and shattering records directly resulting in wins. In the six seasons they played together, Montana and Rice completed 55 scoring passes during the regular season and another 13 in the post season.[†] "We developed a great chemistry, like magic on the football field," Rice said. "We went through so many different situations in practice and in games that we both began to know what we were thinking at all times."[†]

Carefully practiced and constructed, Montana and Rice achieved synergy on the football field – that perfect combination between two entities resulting in a favorable outcome. Synergy is not only applied to sports, it should be applied in the business world as well. In fact, in order for a business to succeed in today's marketplace, a synergy as exemplified by Wal-Mart, needs to exist between the business owner and its' employees.

The Case for Corporate Synergy

The theoretical structure of synergy in the business environment is simple – it is not a new concept. Synergy is the cohesion of the business owner and employee working together toward the same goal – current and future financial security. When both parties have a common goal, a successful partnership is achieved and financial prosperity is reached. A clear understanding and execution of this concept facilitates income development and sustainability. Emerging focus and behavior contributes to the sum and increases the final outcome, goal or object.

G.H. Lewes, a psychologist in the early nineteenth century, was perhaps one of the first to define synergy as an emergent behavior. Lewes coined the term, "emergent" as it relates to "emerging behavior," relating to synergy. According to Lewes, "every resultant is either a sum or a difference of the co-operant forces; their sum, when their directions are the same – their difference, when their directions are contrary."[†] In short, if every resultant (workers and employers) shares the same direction, goals and understanding, the results are the same and the sum is greater. When they differ, they go in opposite directions making it nearly impossible to achieve the end result. Synergy, as it relates to emergent behavior in the business environment, achieves greater success because it leads the two entities down a shared path.

Synergism, in general, may be defined as two entities working together to achieve a favorable result. In the corporate world, this applies when both employer and employee are working toward a common goal. Independently, each entity cannot achieve this without the other, so meshing their individual talents and skills toward the same goal creates synergy and profit. Simply put, the whole is greater than the sum of the individual pieces. Teamwork and a clear understanding of the end goal will result in a better outcome...rather than each working toward the same goal independently.

Abraham Lincoln was an innovator when it came to labor and a model for creating synergy. He recognized an importance in establishing a cohesive relationship between owner and worker, and described capitalism and free market in its simplest terms: "The prudent, penniless beginner in the world, labors for wages awhile, saves a surplus with which to buy tools or land, for himself; the labors on his own account another while, and a length hires another new beginner to help him. This...is free labor—the just and generous system, which opens the way for all."† Business owners begin small, working hard to earn a living and grow his trade. Once he is stable, he hires an assistant or apprentice to grow his business even further.

How Lincoln's Capitalism and Free Market Model may have looked:

1. Businesses creates jobs
2. Employee Works – saves money to start a business
3. Purchasing tools and land – starts a business
4. Labors to build the enterprise – financial stability
5. Hire a new beginner – adds jobs
6. The cycle begins again

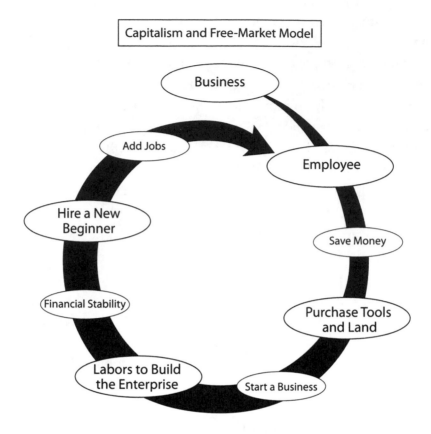

Capitalism and Free-Market Model

Business
Add Jobs
Employee
Hire a New Beginner
Save Money
Financial Stability
Purchase Tools and Land
Labors to Build the Enterprise
Start a Business

Workers are not without risk and contribute to the company's overall bottom line by contributing time and effort. The fact they were hired in the first place means they meet the company's standards, education or skill level for the particular position. In exchange for their time and talent, employees are compensated financially. The company benefits from having someone produce the product that helps their bottom line, and the worker earns compensation, allowing him/her to earn a living. If the worker does not perform their duties up to par and fails to contribute, he or she is in danger of losing their job, and being replaced by someone who is more willing and able to perform the task.

In order for synergy to occur in the workplace, transparency and accountability must be practiced by the employer. Business owners may be hesitant to share sensitive information like profit margins, expenses and income with their employees. Doing so is imperative for the worker to fully understand his place and contribution to the company's bottom line. This background knowledge helps the worker understand his place in the company and shapes his perspective when lobbying for better benefits. Such transparency will also lead to sustainability. If costs are too high, businesses are forced to lay people off and restructure, leaving a negative impact on the employee workforce.

Employees are not just takers. Workers contribute their time and talent for income. This fact alone will help them develop a reasonable perspective when choosing between higher cost benefits. They will realize the possibility that the higher cost will negatively impact the business' ability to grow, to increase wages and to remain competitive in the marketplace.

The Disruption and Destruction of Synergy in the Workplace

The philosophy of establishing a positive synergy in the workplace isn't new and it can easily be obtained. Yet some of America's largest manufacturers and corporations fail to get it. Why? In today's business market, a third variable finds its way into the equation and wreaks havoc on a company's attempt at creating synergy with its employees. I call this the Wedge Model. Labor unions are the wedge between workers and managers. Their intrusion on our workforce not only hinders the chance for success but cripples the economy at large.

Workers and business owners are critical to survival and sustainable growth. In today's business environment, unions do not offer direct value to the common goal of current and future financial security to both critical parties. If anything, they destroy synergism and emergent behavior. Unions unify the worker with a one-sided perspective, adding a layer of distrust and disrespect between the business owner and employee. The union's potentially, well-intentioned behavior becomes a wedge between workers and employers.

The Wedge Model

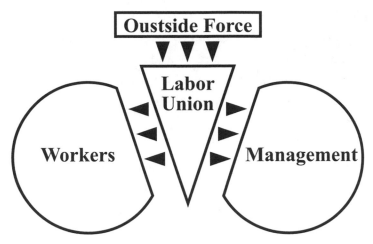

Thanks to the amended Taft-Hartley Act of 1947, an amendment to the Wagner Act of 1935, America's businesses have rescued themselves by relocating themselves to right-to-work states. The Taft-Hartley Act scaled back the power and influence labor unions commonly used for compulsory membership and leveraged employment qualifications. Twenty-two states have legislatively or constitutionally adopted "right-to-work" laws giving the employee the freedom to choose to join a union. Toyota is one example of a corporation taking full advantage of our country's right-to-work states. They locate their manufacturing plants and offices in states where unions have a diminished influence.

General Motors, on the other hand, remains in Michigan – the state most crippled by the effect of unions and its' destructive forces. While multiple factors have led to GM's downfall, one of the most notable is the influence of labor unions and the impact on GM's bottom line.

In light of the recession and the government's bailout of two of the auto industry's "Big Three," the United Auto Workers (UAW) was forced to make concessions with the automaker in order for it to find more capital to continue making cars. One of several compromises the UAW and GM made was the elimination of the "jobs bank," which paid laid-off workers nearly their full wages until they found other jobs or their contract expired. At the date of its elimination, GM's "jobs bank" was paying 85% of the salaries for approximately 1,600 workers. As if the "jobs bank" wasn't enough of a lead weight for a corporation teetering on the brink of bankruptcy under the terms agreed upon with the UAW, GM is stuck paying for the workers who were in the jobs bank before the deal was struck – responsible for 72% of their pay.[†] GM can't win. It's as if the government and supportive American citizens in general, are giving them a second chance to succeed while the unions continue forcing their hand…making GM's restructuring nearly impossible. That's about as far away from synergy as you can get.

To some, unions have served their purpose in our country's growing economy. Others might also argue their efforts have led to better treatment of America's workers; established labor laws, shortened work days and contributed to the establishment of equality in the workplace. But at this time unions have overstayed their welcome. Their presence in today's workforce is disruptive, disparaging and is weighing down attempts to achieve the American Dream.

Growth and Prosperity Through Synergy

Despite the nagging effects unions are forcing on American businesses, many are emerging successfully by implementing a synergistic model in their workplaces.

Cisco Systems, an industry leader in the development of intellectual property (IP) based networking technologies, has been recognized as a model of successful management of employees. Cisco enjoys a high level of employee satisfaction and collaboration. In 2009, they made the top ten in CNN/Fortune Magazine Top 100 Best Places to Work.[†] They used a successful model of synergy to achieve these results. CEO John Chambers emphasizes a combination of employee contribution and collaboration to achieve a recipe of synergy for his company. The result? Satisfied employees and a growing profit over many years. Despite the economic downturn, Cisco is emerging as an even bigger leader in the corporate world with 7% job growth and $26 billion in cash and investments. In Fiscal Year 2008, Cisco's net sales reached $39.5 billion with a net income of $8.5 billion GAAP.

Cisco's successful implementation of synergy can be attributed to a combination of employee input coupled with in-house innovation and cooperation. To begin with, Cisco conducts an annual employee survey that not only assesses employees' overall satisfaction with their work environment, it also tests their knowledge of the company. Cisco reported on their most recent survey, along with an 87% overall satisfaction rating, the Understanding Business Category received a particularly favorable response (85%), the employees demonstrating they have a good grasp of the business. This indicates management is doing a good job of educating employees, and the employees understand management's expectations—to work toward a common goal.

In addition to surveys, Cisco conducts focus groups to keep a pulse on employee satisfaction and to respond to their needs. Focus groups taking place last year addressed issues such as flexible work practices, employee health and family support. As a direct result of employee input, the Cisco LifeConnections Center was built later that same year providing an integrated childcare, fitness and employee health center.

Responding to employees desires and tracking their satisfaction isn't the only way to cultivate synergy. In fact, it's only a piece of the synergy puzzle. Cisco further cemented their commitment to synergy by implementing an innovative tool to gather ideas on how to grow the company and expand profits – a win-win for everyone. Cisco's Emerging Technologies group sponsored a wiki called the Idea Zone, that gave employees a forum for submitting their ideas to build on the ideas of their co-workers. Employees submitted more than 500 ideas including input that led to the development of Cisco's TelePresence solution, one of their most innovative emerging technologies.

Another example of Cisco's commitment to fostering synergy in the workplace is providing employees with direct access to Cisco executives. At a company meeting in March 2008, CFO Frank Calderoni challenged employees to find ways to manage Cisco spending in areas such as travel, training, office supplies and equipment. The goal was to cut spending by $1,000 per employee, saving the company from unnecessary spending and overhead. Calderoni followed up the challenge by posting a blog on Cisco's finance website and intranet homepage. The response was extraordinary. Within the first three hours, Calderoni's challenge garnered 40 responses and more than 250 over the next three months.[†]

Establishing synergy is not rocket science and Cisco's strategy can be easily implemented in companies of all sizes. It took a commitment from management to educate, and to foster communication and expectations with employees, as-well-as to develop the mutual respect and collaborative mentality to achieve it. The results led to a stronger, more productive workforce increasing the company's bottom line— *despite* a recession. Employees are happy as business thrives. All of this was accomplished without the use of a single union representative.

Creating Synergy in the Workplace

Studies have shown when employees are satisfied with their work environment, they perform better in the workplace. One study analyzed nearly 8,000 business units in 36 companies examining the relationship between employee satisfaction and business outcomes via customer satisfaction, productivity, profit, employee turnover and accidents.[†]

In many cases, the contrary directions of the employer and employee are by-products of union intervention. When the employer and employee can put their heads together and work toward a common goal uninterrupted by unions, favorable results are inevitable. The goal is to close the gap by focusing on the common goal and getting both parties to work in the same direction.

I've discussed Wal-Mart and Sam Walton's philosophy of creating a team atmosphere with his associates. He believed sharing Wal-Mart's numbers and financial information with his associates would motivate them to do their job to the best of their abilities. Running the business as an open book was key to his success. Walton wrote, "Sharing information and responsibility is a key to any partnership. It makes people feel responsible and involved…"

General Colin Powell once said, "The day soldiers stop bringing you their problems is the day you have stopped leading them."[†] Working together with your employees/ associates, via solid communication and education, completely eliminates the necessity for labor union involvement.

An eight step process must be followed in order to close the *wedge* and allow the flow of synergy:

1. **Clear Visions and Goals** – Dr. Ordway Twead, a lecturer and author on business management once said, "Leadership is the activity of influencing people to cooperate toward the same goal which they come to find desirable."[†] To be a leader act as a guide, or show the way; it is essential to form visions and goals relevant to an organization. Management must understand that to be 100% relevant to everyone, there must be consideration for everyone's needs and desires. Focus groups, leadership teams and change/control think tanks that include employees, establish ownership and commitment to the outcome. Building a clear vision, with well defined objectives and valued incentives, will set the stage for a motivated workforce and create the framework for a unified "team" effort aimed at a successful outcome. Vision must be articulated in a way that every stakeholder (shareholder, management, worker, etc…) understands the value of success and the repercussions of failure.

2. **The Plan** – Once the organization, company or employer is able to clearly communicate the visions and goals of the

organization, it is mission-critical to develop a focused plan for execution. The plan must incorporate and be consistent with the visions and goals established by leadership. In order to accomplish the desired visions and goals, a properly designed plan will have four major components to assure dynamic execution: 1) Strategy, 2) Tactics, 3) Tools and 4) Timeline. The four components will ensure that the entire organization is centered, with clear instructions and pre-defined expectations, which level the playing field when the organization begins working as a team. It also raises the bar for accountability. As a synergistic team we build momentum and it fosters a better work environment...working together for a common goal!

3. **Communication** – Employers who open the channels of communication generate a better response from workers, which in turn, increases the bottom line. Communicate the intention of working together for a solution. Employees need to feel they are *needed* and *wanted* for the success of the company. Their value within the company needs to be communicated along with the expectations of their duties. It is advantageous for all parties to work together to develop a plan that reaches and accomplishes the "common vision and goal." Once this is clear, confirmed and understood, communicate it to the entire organization. Buy-in from everyone will develop and maintain the momentum for success.

4. **Education** – Teach employees about the impact of their decisions and behavior, not only as it relates to them, but to the company as a whole. Employers and employees alike should recognize that all behavior and decisions will have a direct impact on the final outcome. Clearly articulate their responsibilities to reach the desired outcome. Setting clear and proper expectations for every employee, will help to develop and accelerate momentum. This type of education for the

employee is not a one-time occurrence. It should be practiced regularly in an honest and forthright manner. Transparency develops trust. Information will empower all parties to make clear, informed decisions.

5. **Offer Union Alternatives** – In most cases, union alternatives would fall under education. Throughout American history, unions have done an effective job unifying for the rights of workers. Their efforts have been rewarded with countless labor laws supporting workers' rights. I call the successful passages of labor laws the "evolving substitute" for labor unions. The following is a direct quote from the Department of Labor's website: "The Department of Labor (DOL) administers and enforces more than *180 federal laws*. These mandates and the regulations that implement them cover many workplace activities for about *10 million employers and 125 million workers.*"[†] Workers, if they know their rights under law, are protected from a multitude of abuses from employers. The evolution of labor laws remain the most powerful and lasting basis of support for the worker.

   Below is a sample of the Department of Labor's comprehensive list of laws:

   - Black Lung Benefits Act (BLBA)
   - Consumer Credit Protection Act (CCPA)
   - Contract Work Hours and Safety Standards Act (CWHSSA)
   - Copeland "Anti-Kickback" Act
   - Davis-Bacon and Related Acts (DBRA)
   - Employee Polygraph Protection Act (EPPA)
   - Employee Retirement Income Security Act (ERISA)
   - Energy Employees Occupational Illness Compensation Program Act (EEOICPA)
   - Executive Order 11246

- Fair Labor Standards Act (FLSA)
- Family and Medical Leave Act (FMLA)
- Federal Employees' Compensation Act (FECA)
- Federal Mine Safety and Health Act (Mine Act)
- Immigration and Nationality Act (INA)
- Labor-Management Reporting and Disclosure Act (LMRDA)
- Longshore and Harbor Workers' Compensation Act (LHWCA)
- Mass Transit Employee Protections
- McNamara-O'Hara Service Contract Act (SCA)
- Migrant and Seasonal Agricultural Worker Protection Act (MSPA)
- Occupational Safety and Health (OSH) Act
- Rehabilitation Act of 1973, Section 503
- Uniformed Services Employment and Reemployment Rights Act (USERRA)
- Vietnam Era Veterans' Readjustment Assistance Act (VEVRAA)
- Walsh-Healey Public Contracts Act (PCA)
- Worker Adjustment and Retraining Notification Act (WARN) http://www.dol.gov/compliance/laws/comp-warn.htm
- Whistleblower Protections

Workers have enough life pressure as it relates to their jobs and providing for their families. The constant concern that they may be giving up or relinquishing protection by NOT joining a union, will impact their performance and ownership as it relates to loyalty to the organization. But if they understand that labor laws protect their interests, on all fronts, trust returns and productivity will increase.

Consider this – the taxes we, as Americans, pay to the federal government, make us members of the most powerful union in the world...The Department of Labor.

6. **Return and Report** – "When performance is measured, performance improves. When performance is measured *and* reported, the rate of improvement accelerates."[†] It is one thing to establish clear objectives and expectations for each team member, it is another thing to report on the successes or failures the organization is experiencing given current plan implementation and outcome. Many organizations do a fine job communicating the visions and goals, however, their failures stem from the "team" not understanding the true and final outcome. Not understanding the value or risks associated with their contribution is unnerving and not in sync. Behavior changes when it is measured and communicated. Communication, as mentioned above, is a vital ingredient to accomplishing the best possible outcome. Communication, as mentioned above, comes by way of expectations and then from the workers, reporting their efforts. All workers want to be recognized for their contributions. If you do not recognize team members for their contributions...the unions may have open doors to influence the workers you value. The door only has to be open a crack to feel the impact of unwanted influences.

7. **Recognition and Reward** – Employees need recognition and reward for a job well done. It's simply human nature and cultivating that emotion is crucial for the productivity and output of an employee. A good manager or leader praises a job well done and will reward such hard work with monetary or valued rewards.

8. **Consistency** – One of the most basic principles I have learned in business is the principle of consistency. As it relates to organizational goals and constructing the framework of a synergistic team, consistency offers a level of predictability and

helps to reduce uncertainty and increase morale. Consistency in communicating the vision and goal, expectations, strategies, tactics, tools and timeline for execution must be adopted and endured—through, to the final outcome.

Adhering to these strategies will help businesses form a synergy with employees, that will provide a basis to develop and/or maintain a foundation for a profitable and union- free enterprise. This organization will have the ability to hedge against the unwanted, unneeded and intended influence of today's labor unions. As we've discussed, synergy can only occur when the two entities – the employer and the employee – are in step with one another. It does not involve a third party. Below, is my revised model, which does not include an "outside" force or union involvement. It promotes synergy and unification toward the "common goal." This is a simple model that promotes easy adoption and consistent behavior.

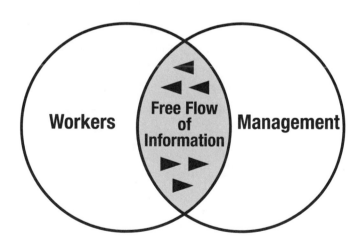

In many cases returning to the simple basics is the best remedy to prevent outright failure.

One word of caution, if you do not consistently maintain open communication with your employees, you begin the process of divergent interests. When there is no communication, you are allowing an opening for the outside force, the wedge – or labor unions, to penetrate your organization. Fair treatment, good communication and consistency will protect the synergy you have worked hard to develop.

Working Together to Accomplish the Best Outcome

Over time, and especially in today's marketplace, unions have placed an extra burden on the system of synergy and threaten to break it. The unions are interrupting the ebb and flow of business and are muddling expectations in order to line their own pockets and agendas. It is time to reclaim our businesses and commit to a model beneficial to both our profitability *and* our treasured employees. The sooner we start acting on this, the sooner our economy will stabilize. The more hands working toward the same objective will lighten the load, accelerate the outcome and build a sustainable future.

† *See appendix for reference.*

"I want to urge devotion to the fundamentals of human liberty – the principles of volunteerism. No lasting gain has ever come from compulsion."
> *– Samuel Gompers*
> *Father of the Labor Movement*

"To give voice, truth and political direction to the American people in the battle against compulsory unionism, this is the purpose of the National Right-to-Work organizations."
> *– Reed Larson*
> *National Right-to-Work Foundation*

CHAPTER TEN

Right-to-Work States

Exhibiting Freedom, Protecting Our
National and State Sovereignty

When we consider economic development within the United States and specifically within individual states, it is important to understand the variables influencing economic growth.

Historically, America has been recognized for leadership, industrial growth, freedom and liberty. The latter two, specifically, have underscored our country's foundation and rise in becoming an uncontested world economic power. Our young nation has worked hard with blood, sweat, triumph and tears to become the most powerful nation in the world. As a nation, we thrive on freedom and the ability to choose our path to success. These fundamental principles act as the catalyst to creativity, innovation and prosperity.

The concept of prosperity has underpinned the motivation behind entrepreneurs, business owners and scientists in the development of our basic standards of living. Much of this has been accomplished through incentive and competition. Competition is a healthy and productive component of our nation's current and future success. Simply put, monetary incentive is capitalism at its best and our capitalistic nation and current infrastructure is an environment ripe for cultivating dreams and improving futures for everyone.

Capitalism is defined as an economic system characterized by private or corporate ownership of capital goods. Other characteristics of capitalism include investments, prices, production, and the distribution of goods, determined by private decision. Capitalism is primarily determined by competition in a free market. The origins of capitalism are deeply rooted in the American economy and stem from the practice of mercantilism in the Middle East during the Middle Ages. In its simplest definition, mercantilism was the distribution of goods in the interest of earning a profit. A vendor would make or purchase his goods at one price and then sell them at a higher price to earn a profit.

Eventually, as Europe's economy and culture evolved, mercantilism evolved into capitalism. While based on the same principle, capitalism became a bit more complex and added an element of labor into the system. The production work, or human labor that is required to produce and distribute a product, becomes wage labor. People began earning wages for their work instead of goods. For a capitalist, the property or product owners' interests lie within the productivity and efficiency with which the product is being produced and sold. Once he is profitable, he can hire more labor. The more labor he hires, the more product he produces, the more profitable he becomes and so on. The division of labor aspect of this became problematic for Europe and America in the nineteenth and twentieth centuries because as more and more people were hired to work, the focus on individual output decreased and wages were lowered as a result.

As a whole, the concept of capitalism is highly individualistic in that the person earning the profit is driven to do so by his own interests and incentives. To thrive, capitalism relies on a consumer culture. People must be available and willing to purchase goods as well as produce them. Their willingness to purchase products at certain prices determines a product's price point and a capitalist's ability to turn a profit. This "economic freedom" is widely celebrated in this country and has proven to be extremely successful for millions of people with an array of varying financial success.[†]

There is no doubt in my mind that economic growth, spurred on by capitalism, launched this country into becoming the world power it is. While abuses have been made in the past by capitalists, wrongs have been corrected and righteousness has prevailed. Laws protect workers from abuses and capitalists now work *with* workers to create better lives for all. From a businesses perspective, taking into account the benefits for workers, their well-being and ability to prosper, capitalism is invaluable.

Incentive, the desire and need to produce and sell a product, by way of capitalism, is what makes people and businesses successful.

Ben Bernanke, Chairman of the United States Federal Reserve Board, described the importance of incentive when analyzing productivity during his remarks to the Greater Omaha Chamber of Commerce in February 2007. Bernanke said, "Although we Americans strive to provide equality of economic opportunity, we do not guarantee equality of economic outcomes, nor should we. Indeed, without the possibility of unequal outcomes tied to differences in effort and skill, the economic incentive for productive behavior would be eliminated, and our market-based economy – which encourages productive activity primarily through the promise of financial reward – would function far less effectively."[†]

Bernanke understands economic incentive, in a market-based economy, enhances productive behavior and financial rewards. In a competitive marketplace, capital, businesses, employees and consumers look for an advantage. The advantage sought centers on free markets and profitability. Free markets open doors for elevated potential returns on capital, greater profitability for businesses, higher wages for employees, more jobs and added choices for consumers. When will we, as a country, step back and embrace the truth…that the success our nation has experienced is founded on a free-market based economy?

Let me be clear. I am a capitalist and support its fundamentals wholeheartedly. But it is important that prosperity not come at the expense or abuse of someone's human rights and fair treatment. Our country has fought dearly to establish and protect the First Amendment to the Constitution which states:

"Congress shall make no law respecting an establishment of religion, or prohibiting the free exercise thereof; or abridging the freedom of speech, or of the press; or the right of the people peaceably to assemble, and to petition the Government for a redress of grievances."

From our nation's earliest founders who laid down their lives to establish these freedoms, to today's soldiers serving in America's armed forces, millions have sacrificed their lives fighting to protect it. We simply cannot let it slip away or allow any sort of group or entity to infringe on our constitutional rights.

But they are. Our rights are being violated and our First Amendment protection is being threatened. Our nation, as it directly relates to the work force, has slowly compromised free choice and independent protection of the law by way of labor unions.

Union officials, the organizations who preach their protection of the worker, the so-called unified voice who proclaim they work for the American labor force, are deceptively and deliberately limiting our freedom, human rights and civil liberties.

Compulsion and the Threat to Our Unalienable Rights

It is important prosperity not come at the expense or abuse of someone's human rights and fair treatment. As I've noted, the merits of labor unions continue to be debated among workers, employers and the public. In a recent poll conducted by the Associated Press, the majority of Americans are wary of union influence and compulsion. A union's ability to force membership upon workers, using compulsory means and *collective bargaining* as a condition of employment, is both dishonest and un-American. I join critics in questioning these tactics and find their infringement on workers' rights an absolute atrocity. It undermines our First Amendment protection and reeks of dishonesty.

Unions often swoop in to help arrange collective bargaining agreements between public sector employees and the governments they work for. The non-member employees pay the union to be their representative, knowing the union often has the know-how and tactics to win over better pay or benefits. This, on the surface, makes sense. Everyday, people pay broker fees to enter into a negotiating table they know little about. When purchasing a home, people consult a real-estate broker. When developing a will, one may turn to an estate planning attorney. When trying to invest money in capital markets, one would retain the services of an investment professional. All of these individuals are well versed, trained and licensed in their respective fields to assist those in need. For sharing their training and knowledge, these brokers are given a fee or a commission directly related to their work.

Leave it to unions to overstep those boundaries when it comes to money. Non-members, who retained the negotiating services of unions in Washington, were concerned their fees paid to the union would be going to more than just negotiating services. In fact, it was well known the unions were using their negotiating fees to support union-backed candidates in political races. This outraged the non-members who thought their money was for a service, not for a *buy-in* into the union way of life. The workers took action, calling upon the Washington state legislature to draft what is known as "Section 760," which required unions to get an affirmative authorization from non-members to use their fees (NOT DUES) in election-related purposes. When it was found that the Washington Education Association was violating this law, two lawsuits were brought against the union. The union fought this, actually claiming Section 760 violated *their* First Amendment rights and not the other way around.

The U.S. Supreme Court, however, saw the matter for what it was. The First Amendment doesn't give people, or unions, for that matter, the right to do whatever they want as an organization. If non-members pay a fee-for-service, they are not buying into the union, nor are they supporting pro-union candidates. The money does not belong to the union to spend as the unions please. The money is for negotiating a better collective bargaining agreement and nothing else.

In this case, unions were distorting the First Amendment – violating the rights of non-member workers. It would be comparable to an attorney getting paid to make a will for a couple, getting the money up front, and then using that money to work on his own will instead of the work he was hired to do. It violates the rights of the couple, just as the unions were violating the rights of non-member workers who thought they had paid for a service, not an election. Supporting cases include Aboud v. Detroit Board Of Education and Teachers v. Hudson, both of which required unions to give non-members the right to opt-out or opt-in to certain expenditures outside the scope of the original negotiating agreement.

One could even make the argument that the unions were, in fact, violating the First Amendment rights of the non-member employees. They were distorting voices without consent, into support for electoral issues they would not have supported otherwise. Thankfully, with three separate U.S. Supreme Court decisions, unions can no longer blatantly overstep the boundaries of the U.S. Constitution for their own ends.

In addition to misusing membership fees, labor unions have been cited in multiple incidences involving workers' struggles to maintain their jobs while holding fast to their religious, personal and or political values. Mark Fischer and Robert P. Hunter, writers for the Mackinac Center for Public Policy, wrote an article entitled, "First Amendment Challenges to Forced Union Membership." The excerpt on the following page demonstrates workers' struggles in maintaining their freedom of religion while unions flex their muscle and punish those who challenge them.

Prior to the 1972 amendment of the Civil Rights Act, the Act did not present itself as the best legal basis to sue a union on behalf of private-sector employers, whose religious rights had been violated. Such litigants more commonly used the First Amendment's guarantee of free exercise of religion, in an effort to get unions to accommodate their religious beliefs. These efforts were largely unsuccessful.

Two typical cases are *Gray v.Gulf, Mobile & Ohio Railroad Co.22 and Linscott v. Millers Falls Co. 23*. In the case of Gray, a Seventh Day Adventist, he refused to join the railroad union because of religious convictions. This constituted a violation of a union security clause requiring employees to become union members within 60 days of employment. This individual rejected the union's offer to permit him to pay an agency fee and forgo formal union membership.

The railroad then terminated Gray as called for in the collective bargaining agreement. Gray sued on several constitutional grounds, including the First Amendment's free exercise clause to no avail. Both the trial and appellate courts ruled against Gray.

Likewise, in the *Linscott* case – Beatrice Linscott a Seventh Day Adventist, refused to join the union due to her religious convictions. Instead, she offered to pay an amount equivalent to her unions dues and initiation fees to a non-religious charity. The union refused and discharged Linscott. She sued the union on grounds of a violation of First Amendment protection but lost at both the trail and appellate levels. The court's justification was outrageous. The appellate court concluded the government's interest in maintaining a peaceful labor relations climate outweighed the burden imposed on Linscott to protect her religious sensibilities.[†]

These cases demonstrate unions are infringing on not just workers' rights, but *American's* rights, by taking away First Amendment protection. Not since the 1700s, have we experienced this type of behavior and the worst part is, they are getting away with it.

While it is not expressly written into the Constitution, Freedom of Association is protected under the First Amendment. This can refer to legal bans on private contracts, negotiated between private employers and their employees, requiring workers to join a union as a term and condition of employment. Supporters of this sort of private freedom of association claim the right to join a union incorporates a right *not* to join a union and this is supported by right-to-work laws.

Compulsory Membership and the Right-to-Work

Forcing someone to adopt, accept or support another's political or moral perspective is wrong and fundamentally contradicts the United States Constitution. Equally disloyal to the constitution would be eliminating a worker's ability to organize or join a union.

Years ago, the National Right to Work Foundation published a phenomenal book written by Reed Larson titled, *Stranglehold: How Union Bosses Have Hijacked Our Government*. The abridged edition, a mere 100 pages in length, is chock-full of information and examples of how present-day unions have been and continue to be a detriment to society. To organize in the first place, union bosses must persuade already fixed workers to establish collective bargaining at a company. Thus, if a majority of workers voting in an election choose union representation, it's decided for the whole company. So, if 51 percent of *employees who vote*, vote for a union and 49 percent vote against, *all* workers are subject to union representation or "exclusive representation." Larson views unions' compulsory means to acquire membership as one example of unions' stranglehold on society. In fact, he calls it the forced unionism "two-step" where monopoly bargaining and forced payments of dues comprise two steps.

Here's how it works. Larson writes, the union's term "exclusive representation" should be more accurately described as "monopoly bargaining." Union bosses have a monopoly on bargaining in the workplace whether the particular worker wants it or not. The second step involves union bosses turning to elected officials for funding. They are so heavily burdened, and argue they are forced to represent workers who don't pay for the "exclusive representation" they enforce. (Larson)

Unions are dancing this two-step while talking out of both sides of their mouth.

Presently, unions are crossing the line even more with the Employee Free Choice Act, which clearly uses compulsory means to pad their membership logs and increase their bank accounts. This practice is shamefully perverse and trounces on our workers' rights and civil liberties.

Our nation is in the middle of a terrible economic downturn. For years, we have seen businesses and jobs migrate outside our country and from state to state. Often, a business' migration stems from its need for survival, growth, profitability and to escape outside forces which limits its freedoms to do what is best for business, workers and communities in which they serve.

There has been a similar migration with respect to the overall population of our country. People must also survive and as businesses close up shop and relocate to areas that promote greater profitability... the dependent population follows. The population base is searching to maintain or improve their standard of living. In many cases, this migratory population has been impacted by manufacturing migration and is interested in the simple principle of financial security. This anomaly is best demonstrated when we consider states with business-friendly climates.

For years, heated debate has surrounded right-to-work laws and policies. Arguments have centered on collective bargaining, forced union membership, job growth, business migration and the pure economic impact on workers, wages, employers and our states' economies. While debate is good, it's often misguided.

Unfortunately, most citizens are unaware of what "right-to-work" means or the implications if such a law is passed. Roland Zullo, a research scientist for the Institute for Labor and Industrial Relations at the University of Michigan wrote. "...the term, right-to-work is a misnomer. Right-to-work has nothing to do with the right of a person to seek and accept gainful employment."

Zullo is right and touches on an important point. Many Americans are misinformed about right-to-work laws and what is covered.

According to the National Right-to-Work Legal Defense Foundation, the general concept of *right-to-work* is defined as laws that "secure the right of employees to decide for themselves whether or not to join or financially support a union."[†] Under these laws however, workers in the airline and railway industries are exempt.

Right-to-work statutes give states the ability to enact right-to-work laws. These laws were found in the Taft-Hartley Act. They also prohibit employers from making membership hinge on an individual's hiring or employment status. Prior to its passing, employers under the National Labor Relations Act could declare themselves a "closed shop" and require employees to become union members. Although the Act prohibits "closed shops" from existing, it does allow "union shops," where an employee is required to become a member of a union or else his/her job is in peril. The Act allows for states to prohibit "union shops" from existing. Twenty two states are right-to-work states with varying statutes of worker protection.[†]

Do You Live in a Right-to-Work State?

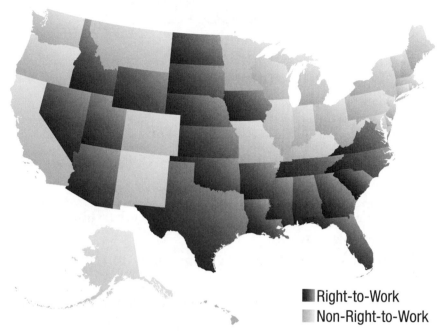

■ Right-to-Work
▨ Non-Right-to-Work

The legal definition of "right-to-work" can be summed up as, "Under federal labor law and state right-to-work laws, which exist in slightly less than half of the states, you have the right to resign from membership in a union at any time. If you resign from membership, you may not be able to participate in union elections or meetings, vote in collective bargaining ratification elections or participate in other "internal" union activities. If you resign, you cannot be disciplined by the union for any post-resignation conduct."[†]

The Taft-Hartley Act also authorizes individual states to outlaw the union and agency shops with the exception of local governments such as cities or counties.

Arizona is an example of one of five right-to-work states where an employee's right-to-work is established under the state constitution and not under legislative action. Below, I have included the Arizona Right- to-Work Article from the state's constitution.

ARIZONA

Ariz. Const. art. XXV
Title 23. Labor
Chapter 8. Labor Relations
Article 1. Right-to-Work
ARTICLE 1. RIGHT-TO-WORK

Right to work or employment without membership in labor organization.

No person shall be denied the opportunity to obtain or retain employment because of non-membership in a labor organization, nor shall the State or any subdivision thereof, or any corporation, individual or association of any kind enter into any agreement, written or oral, which excludes any person from employment or continuation of employment because of non-membership in a labor organization. (Addition approved election Nov. 5, 1946, eff. Nov. 25, 1946; amended November 30, 1982.)

Below is a legislative example of right-to-work law for the state of North Carolina.

NORTH CAROLINA

CHAPTER 95. DEPARTMENT OF LABOR AND LABOR REGULATIONS
ARTICLE 10.
DECLARATION OF POLICY AS TO LABOR ORGANIZATIONS.
N.C. Gen. Stat. §§ 95-78. to 84.

§ 95-78. Declaration of public policy.

The right to live includes the right to work. The exercise of the right to work must be protected and maintained free from undue restraints and coercion. It is hereby declared to be the public policy of North Carolina that the right of persons to work shall not be denied or abridged on account of membership or nonmembership in any labor union or labor organization or association. (Enacted March 18, 1947.)

§ 95-79. Certain agreements declared illegal.

Any agreement or combination between any employer and any labor union or labor organization whereby persons not members of such union or organization shall be denied the right to work for said employer, or whereby such membership is made a condition of employment or continuation of employment by such employer, or whereby any such union or organization acquires an employment monopoly in any enterprise, is hereby declared to be against the public policy and an illegal combination or conspiracy in restraint of trade or commerce in the State of North Carolina. (Enacted March 18, 1947.)

§ 95-80. Membership in labor organization as condition of employment prohibited.

No person shall be required by an employer to become or remain a member of any labor union or labor organization as a condition of employment or continuation of employment by such employer. (Enacted March 18, 1947.)

§ 95-81. Nonmembership as condition of employment prohibited.

No person shall be required by an employer to abstain or refrain from membership in any labor union or labor organization as a condition of employment or continuation of employment. (Enacted March 18, 1947.)

§ 95.82. Payment of dues as condition of employment prohibited.

No employer shall require any person, as a condition of employment or continuation of employment, to pay any dues, fees, or other charges of any kind to any labor union or labor organization. (Enacted March 18, 1947.)

§ 95-83. Recovery of damages by persons denied employment.

Any person who may be denied employment or be deprived of continuation of his employment in violation of G.S. 95-80, 95-81 and 95-82 or of one or more of such sections, shall be entitled to recover from such employer and from any other person, firm, corporation, or association acting in concert with him by appropriate action in the courts of this State such damages as he may have sustained by reason of such denial or deprivation of employment. (Enacted March 18, 1947.)

§ 95-84. Application of Article.

The provisions of this Article shall not apply to any lawful contract in force on the effective date hereof but they shall apply in all respects to contracts entered into thereafter and to any renewal or extension of any existing contract. (Enacted March 18, 1947.)

ARTICLE 12

UNITS OF GOVERNMENT AND LABOR UNIONS, TRADE UNIONS, AND LABOR ORGANIZATIONS, AND PUBLIC EMPLOYEE STRIKES

§ 95-98. Contracts between units of government and labor unions, trade unions or labor organizations concerning public employees declared to be illegal.

Any agreement, or contract, between the governing authority of any city, town, county, or other municipality, or between any agency, unit, or instrumentality thereof, or between any agency, instrumentality, or institution of the State of North Carolina, and any labor union, trade union, or labor organization, as bargaining agent for any public employees of such city, town, county or other municipality, or agency or instrumentality of government, is hereby declared to be against the public policy of the State, illegal, unlawful, void and of no effect.(Enacted 1959.)

§ 95-100. No provisions of Article 10 of Chapter 95 applicable to units of government or their employees.

The provisions of Article 10 of Chapter 95 of the General Statutes shall not apply to the State of North Carolina or any agency, institution, or instrumentality thereof or the employees of same nor shall the provisions of Article 10 of Chapter 95 of the General Statutes apply to any public employees or any employees of any town, city, county or other municipality or the agencies or instrumentalities thereof, nor shall said Article apply to employees of the State or any agencies, instrumentalities or institutions thereof or to any public employees whatsoever. (Enacted 1959.)

Constitutionally and legislatively based right-to-work laws are still exposed to the potential of change and amendments. Even though constitutionally based right-to-work laws have greater protection, it is critical for survival that states adopt or add right-to-work laws.

Arguments Against Right-to-Work Laws

As a business owner and fiscal policy expert, I've heard a gambit of arguments against right-to-work laws and, quite frankly, they are misguided and unfounded. Opponents have argued these laws open the door for an opportunity to create a "free rider" problem where a worker, who is not paying union dues, benefits from collective bargaining. They argue that not requiring workers to pay dues significantly diminishes the union's funding source and ability to operate within the workplace. Critics also say right-to-work laws prevent free contracts between unions and business owners.

When considering right-to-work laws and enactments stemming from the Taft-Hartley Act, it isn't difficult to surmise special interest entities such as the National Right-To-Work Legal Defense Foundation and National Right to Work Committee, or even the United States Chamber of Commerce would continue pressing hard for right-to-work legislation. Critics argue their funding and support derives from wealthy industrialists and diminishes their promise to lobby on behalf of the worker or "little guy." Lastly, opponents of right-to-work laws argue unions are significantly weakened by these laws and worker safety and compensation are compromised.

I beg to differ and below I would like to dispell any of the above arguments.

Employees become free riders – As it relates to the "free rider" argument, if an employee joins an organization with collective bargaining benefits he or she still maintains the right to join the union. Now, in this case, the employee has the ability to support perceived value. If the employee has the perception the union garnered him benefits he enjoys, the employee maintains the freedom to choose to participate by paying dues and signing his name to a union card. Maintaining the freedom to choose is key. Additionally, it is important to note if an employee is added to an organization, generally speaking, he has earned the job by his own merits, skills and accomplishments. Forcing union membership clearly demonstrates the true free-rider is the union. The union is a direct benefactor from compulsory membership and revenue from dues. Since when is it okay to force someone to participate in something? When did our country become so lax in its ideals and standards to allow such behavior to slowly smolder until erupting into an outright violation of our rights and liberties?

Outlawing compulsory union dues makes unions less sustainable – This is actually a perfect statement to support the argument for free markets. Generally speaking, the market will sustain value. If workers, in an effort to improve their standard of living and to accomplish current and future financial security feel union membership would help their individual needs or add value, unions would not need to require membership in the first place. They would not need it to "sustain" their activities. If what they offered was so great, workers would join in droves. Forcing workers to join is shameful and an indication of unions' reduced value.

Consider this quote from Samuel Gompers, the so-called Father of the Labor Movement and founder and president of the American Federation of Labor:

"I want to urge devotion to the fundamentals of human liberty – the principles of volunteerism. No lasting gain has ever come from compulsion."

"...No lasting gain has ever come from compulsion."

Gompers understood compulsion will ultimately fail because of a lack of true, motivated support. Compulsion impacts a person's human liberties and freedom and such behavior goes against the grain of lasting success, not to mention the fundamental premise of the United States Constitution. Businesses, people and overall populations have demonstrated their dislike for infringement on their freedoms with change. If we don't like something, we do something about it. We change our jobs, location, wages, workforce, etc. Our nation was founded on the principle of freedom not compulsion.

Right-to-work laws prevent free contracts between unions and business owners – this argument amazes me because the fact is, right-to-work laws do nothing to prevent free contracts between unions and business owners. I completely disagree with the notion that right-to-work laws impede or prevent free contracts. This argument is downright offensive given the fact we live in "Free America." If nothing else, right-to-work laws offer business owners the ability to stand on level ground. They eliminate or reduce the fear of strong-armed intimidation tactics and allow additional freedoms for the worker. These freedoms include participating or not participating in a union. They allow individual, principle-based decisions and choices. Any agreement between a union and a business owner on level ground, should have a fair and equitable outcome.

Let me be clear. I support the right for labor to organize. I support worker's rights. If a labor union is able to organize within a company or an organization on the virtue of perceived necessity of the workers, I support that right. Not compulsion.

Wages are lowered by right-to-work laws – this is another emotional argument. There are two very real facts as it relates to right-to-work laws, wages and jobs. Right-to-work states are growing wages at a faster rate than non-right-to-work states. Additionally, right-to-work states' per-capita income is up and job growth is significantly higher than non-right-to-work states.[†] With continuing job loss and attrition within non-right-to-work states, there is little substantial fact to support this argument.

Policy that supports jobs, financial independence, increased standard of living, sustainable growth and the once well-defined American Dream is the only way to rekindle our nation's economic leadership. Information empowers us to choose the right path to follow, and considering all the facts and history, right-to-work is the right path for our country.

Unions and their supporters resort to emotional finger-pointing and meaningless arguments when referring to the financial fundraising of right-to-work supporters. Whereas proponents of both right-to-work laws and non-right-to-work laws are funded by their constituents. Unions specifically, have been able to maintain a very visible trend of support toward pro-union politicians and other special interests aligned with their mission, by using compulsory or forced dues to further their agenda. As such, any arguments around money and special interest contributions are trivial.

It is clear which policy supports jobs, financial independence, increased standard of living, sustainable growth and the once well-defined American Dream.

The Undeniable Truth:

The Evolution of Right-to-Work States

As I've said, right-to-work states are more profitable and stable than non-right-to-work states and abundant research and analysis supports this statement.

In 1977, David A Williams, an economist for the Heritage Foundation, sought to economically justify the existence of right-to-work laws using major economic indicators revolving around the manufacturing industry. His article, *Right-to-work Laws: Is There Economic Justification for Them?* came to conclusions inferred largely from the Fantus Company, Inc. At the time of his work, the Fantus Company was the largest plant location consulting firm in the world. Part of their work involved using data from the U.S. Labor and Census Bureau to help identify states with the best economic outlook. Fantus studies were often used by clients to identify opportunities for businesses interested in expanding their investments and/or operations.

Upon analyzing Fantus' data, Williams compiled data specific to the manufacturing, construction and non-agricultural/non-farm jobs as well as income statistics and the overall statewide economic benefits of right-to-work laws. Williams was able to show, using this data spanning from 1964 to 1974, that states with right-to-work laws were the beneficiaries of an economic boom; conversely, he proved states whose laws did not give both labor and employers the protection of right-to-work laws were left to languish in dire economic straits, witnessing attrition on all fronts. Very clearly, his study demonstrated right-to-work laws were a consistent and predictable trait offering a foundation for growth.

On the next page, I have included a table of his findings and his facts-based argument around the economic justification of right-to-work laws:

Manufacturing Employment	1964	1974	Actual Gain	% Gain
-RTW States Average	195,200	278,000	83.600	43%
-NRTW States Average	424,100	460,500	36,400	9%
Construction Employment	1964	1974	Actual Gain	% Gain
-RTW States Average	47,900	78,200	30,300	63%
-NRTW States Average	66,100	78,310	12,210	18%
Non-Agricultural Employment	1964	1974	Actual Gain	% Gain
-RTW States Average	757,700	1,170,800	413,100	55%
-NRTW States Average	1,368,710	1,446,980	390,770	29%
Weekly Earnings of Manufacturing Workers	1964	1974	Actual Gain	% Gain
-RTW States Average	$94.44	$156.58	$62.14	40%
-NRTW States Average	$105.50	$181.24	$75.14	42%
Per Capita Personal Income	1964	1974	Actual Gain	% Gain
-RTW States Average	$2,136	$4,819	$2,683	126%
-NRTW States Average	$2,606	$5,469	$2,863	110%
New Housing Units Authorized	1964	1974	Actual Gain	% Gain
-RTW States Average	19,399	22,126	2,727	14%
-NRTW States Average	29,601	20,603	-8,998	-30%
Capital Expenditures	1964	1974	Actual Gain	% Gain
-RTW States Average	$288,530,000	$406,600,000	$118,100,000	41%
-NRTW States Average	$499,470,000	$601,060,000	$100,590,000	20%

RTW = Right-To-Work   NRTW = Non-Right-To-Work

US Bureau of Labor Statistics

Look carefully at each of the macro categories and you will see ecliptic growth from the right-to-work states. In most cases, job growth in manufacturing, construction and non-agricultural segments of right-to-work states doubles the growth in non-right-to-work states. Superior job growth leads to faster per capita income growth, new housing and capital expenditures. Economic growth in all major categories is good for the worker, company and communities. Of his findings, Williams concludes, "…it is fairly obvious that rather than impairing economic growth, right-to-work laws produce an economic climate that facilitates prosperity to employees, employers and the entire community."[†]

Freedom Promotes Prosperity

Through my company, RG Capital, LLC, a company that succeeds or fails by interpreting economic outcomes, I have commissioned a study to analyzes data to determine present-day benefits to right-to-work laws. Using many of the same indicators and taking into account present day findings, I attempted to prove states that have right-to-work laws are reaping continuous economic benefits, not just over the past decade, but over the past generation.

The results were overwhelmingly positive and in favor of right-to-work protection.

In fact, using data from the 1960s well into present day, my study proves one underlying factor leading to economic success for employees, employers and the overall state economy, is the presence of right-to-work protection.

Right-to-work critics argue income tax and other economic variables, as factors contributing to the widening gap of economic prosperity between non-right-to-work and right-to-work states. In some sense, they are right regarding the economic variables; however my careful analysis and research proved economic benefits were cultivated and maintained as a result of right- to-work protection.

As we've seen, right-to-work protection is the foundation upon which workers, businesses and capital investment can build and flourish. Additionally, my research shows a trend demonstrating right-to-work laws attract manufacturing, add jobs, increase a state's population base, generate additional tax revenue, lower tax rates and augments economic security for residents. Across the board, it's a win-win situation. The old adage that people will "talk with their feet" is clearly demonstrated with our findings. Right-to-work means the *right-to-grow* and the *right-to-prosper*.

For nearly four decades, there has been significant net increase in capital expenditures for manufacturing in right-to-work states. Capital expenditures are a significant indicator because they reflect plant improvements in manufacturing industries, rather than simply repairs

Net Growth in Capital Expenditures 1967 - 2004	
Non Right-to-work	366%
Right-to-work	598%

US Census Bureau; Census of Manufacturers

and maintenance. Through accounting figures, capital expenditures show a company's willingness to invest in plants in order to expand production in the future. This expansion creates jobs and future opportunities for more workers to find sustainable labor and create a career in manufacturing.

As such, the numbers presented here are quite noteworthy. While non-right-to-work states have seen growth of 366% in capital expenditures, right-to-work states have seen their capital expenditure growth rate nearly double that at 598%, clearly eclipsing the growth in non-right-to-work states. Right-to-work laws have created an environment in which the net investment made by companies in their manufacturing plants can be considerably larger when they know the state's economic settings allow for it.

Over time, these investments not only allow for more production and efficiency from plants, they also allow companies to employ more people within the states. When one compares states with right-to-work laws against those with a non-right-to-work status, the conclusions of David Williams are again upheld. Shown on the next page, a net growth in manufacturing jobs was only found in right-to-work states over the past 30 years. Non-right-to-work states suffered from a statistical hemorrhage of manufacturing jobs over the same scope of time.

Capital expenditures are not the only factor contributing to manufacturing job increases in right-to-work states. The reality remains, American manufacturing companies are moving into states where both the worker and the employer are treated fairly. Companies that rely heavily on labor consistently move out of states that have economic environments hazardous to the sustainable health of the company.

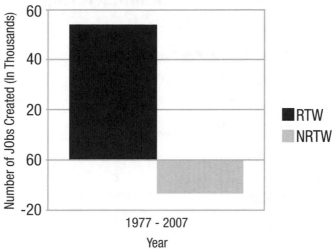

Net Growth of Manufacturing Jobs – RTW vs NRTW

US Census Bureau; Census of Manufacturers

A glaring example of this situation is best articulated in an article written on March 3, 2008 for the Wall Street Journal Online, in the editorial, "Texas v. Ohio, Centered on Free Trade and Right-to-Work Laws."

The article explains, "…Texas has gained 36,000 manufacturing jobs since 2004 and has ranked as the nation's top exporting state for six years in a row. Its $168 billion in exports in 2007 translate into tens of thousands of jobs. Ohio, Indiana and Michigan are losing auto jobs, but many of these "runaway plants" are not fleeing to China, Mexico or India. Instead, they've moved to more business-friendly U.S. states, including Texas. GM recently announced plans for a new plant to build hybrid cars. Guess where? Near Dallas. In 2006, the Lone Star State exported $5.5 billion cars and trucks to Mexico and $2.4 billion vehicles to Canada."

The article further points out that Texas, as a right-to-work state, has built 1,000 new plants and has added more than 340,000 jobs since 2005. Companies like Microsoft, Samsung and Fujitsu, along with other foreign companies, now call Texas home.[t]

Relocating companies bring capital, other businesses and jobs to

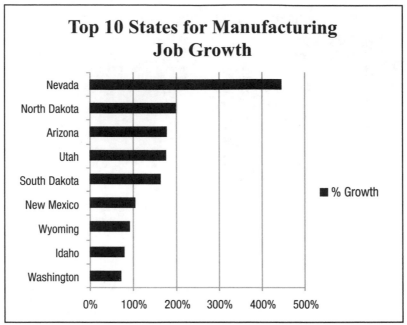

Top 10 States for Manufacturing Job Growth

US Census Bureau

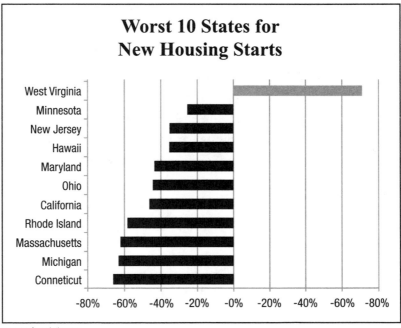

Worst 10 States for New Housing Starts

www.taxfoundation.org

the state. States with non-right-to-work laws are not only impeding the progress of companies, they are impeding the growth of jobs so desperately needed by states' residents.

Sam Gompers, the founding father of the labor movement would be disgusted with how unions have evolved. The unions, that once sought to offer protection and safeguards for the American worker, are now consumed in greed; hiding behind a mask of activism and misleading hard-working Americans. After all, it was Gompers who said, "… No lasting gain has ever come from compulsion." If union membership is about the unified voice, building a stronger team and a "members first" mentality, then it should be acceptable to unions to comply with a worker's wishes to remain union-free. Instead, the focus has become centered around membership dues – a far cry from its original mission. My understanding is, unions were organized by the workers for the workers. Dues were merely a byproduct, stemming from the necessity to operate the union programs and infrastructure, for the workers. Today's unions have become drunk with power and are abusing laws, defending their ability to organize, and taking advantage of the workers they claim to protect.

Taking into account all of the facts surrounding today's labor unions, it is accurate to surmise unions—the proverbial apples, have fallen far from the tree from which its roots were firmly planted. Gompers' progeny has been dismantled, and its current existence is tearing apart our economy; one job and one worker at a time.

Non-Right-to-Work Employees

Arguments supporting a right-to-work landscape are rich with proof. Americans who are employed in non-right-to-work states work more hours for less money. That's right – according to my research, right-to-work employees work an average of six FEWER days each year. The right-to-work employees' burden is lighter than it would be, had they been living and working in a non-right-to-work state.

How does this work?

Jobs are far more than a means by which a plant produces product and a laborer provides money for him or her. Jobs represent dollars to help build and protect a state's infrastructure. Jobs represent economic security for a state's residents. More, higher-paying jobs with sustainable companies can lead states to an increase in overall revenue without overburdening the residents who have lived there for years. Citizens of right-to-work states consistently work fewer days to pay for their taxes every year.[†]

The following chart illustrates the fact that year-over-year non-right-to-work employees must work an average of 6 more days each year to pay for the suffocating burden of higher taxes.

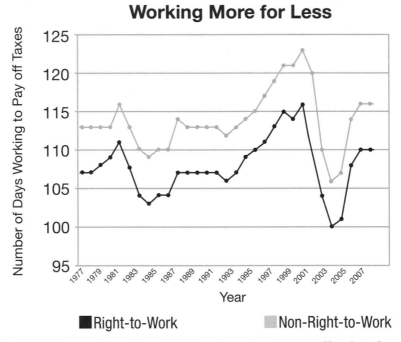

Working More for Less

Right-to-Work   Non-Right-to-Work

The AFL-CIO claims they are the "single most effective force in America for enabling working people to build better lives and futures for (our) families."[†] Really?! How can they enable people to build better lives and futures when they support policies that cause their members to work harder for less compensation?

These poor souls are working just has hard, if not harder than their right-to-work brethren, yet their standards of living are much lower. How is that protecting the worker? How is he getting his fair share? He's not and it's because unions have lost their way and have become so infatuated with greed and power they've forgotten what it's like to protect and serve the very members who keep them employed. It is time America's workforce comes together to stop these greedy unions and take back what is rightfully ours…the right-to-work and prosper.

† See appendix for reference.

"The government's view of the economy could be summed up in a few short phrases: If it moves, tax it. If it keeps moving, regulate it. And if it stops moving, subsidize it."

– Ronald Reagan

CHAPTER ELEVEN

Lower Taxes = Higher Revenue

A Flawed Equation

It is counter intuitive to think lower taxes will actually increase a state's or the nation's tax revenue. It's hard to imagine a situation where less tax revenue being generated in a state would result in increasing a state's income. Politicians often fall into this way of thinking and real, economic solutions are overlooked. They focus on looking for short term, immediate gratification solutions or, plainly, they do not have the experience to see beyond the NOW.

When faced with budget shortfalls, often, their shortsighted perspective formulates a crude equation...higher taxes = higher revenue. This equation is flawed. Their erroneous perspective is hopeful that the potential for higher revenue will be the saving grace to budgetary constraints and deficits. Even though history has demonstrated that populations and businesses within a community will migrate away from cannibalistic tax policy, lawmakers continually push for the perceived *quick fix* by raising taxes. Supporting numerous research evaluations, my study reinforces the value of right-to-work laws, lower taxations and more jobs for American workers.

Further articulating the notion that forced membership strains financial outcomes of both workers and businesses (governments fall into the business category, too) is the fact that since compulsory unionism exploded in the government sector, taxes at all levels have skyrocketed. Larson's *Stranglehold* attests that "after adjusting for inflation, from 1970 to 1995, taxes leaped 80 percent at the federal level and nearly 90 percent at the state and local level." Government gets their revenue from taxes and when the going gets tough and state coffers are running dry, politicians are faced with three options: raise taxes, cut spending or go into debt. Given our country's track record and current jaw-dropping $1.4 trillion deficit, you can figure out which path these ill-advised lawmakers choose time and time again.[†]

In the book, *Rich States, Poor States*, authors Laffer, Moore and Williams point out the reality that people move from high tax jurisdictions. Their book thoroughly illustrates the "migration factor" and its relative impact on economies. One example, from their book, centers on Maryland lawmakers recently doubling cigarette taxes to $2.00 per pack. Lawmakers were hopeful that the increased tax would generate additional revenue to support healthcare and help to eliminate their growing deficit. What was the outcome? Laffer, Moore, and Williams wrote, "…they [Maryland lawmakers] were sorely mistaken, as The Wall Street Journal reports that cigarette sales are down 25 percent. In fact, nearly 30 million fewer cigarettes have been sold in Maryland since the tax increase this year."[†]

Taxation hurts economies. This decision did not help the state of Maryland and actually put downward pressure on its already deteriorating resources. It hurt citizens instead of helping them. There is no way to accurately measure the ancillary impact on the state of Maryland for this taxation. Possibly other goods and services once purchased by residents of Maryland, are being sacrificed while smokers are on these "cigarette field trips." The guy who goes to a convenience store for a pack of cigarettes likely grabs a soda and bag of chips. Not only is the cigarette revenue gone, so is the other spending. This means less revenue going into state coffers and more hardship on citizens and on businesses. Think of all the other incidents similar to this, where local governments raised taxes with the hopes of generating income...and it backfired!

Newton's third law of motion has to be recognized... *"For every action, there is an equal; an opposite reaction."* Lawmakers must adopt a broader perspective than the myopic considerations of law. They must understand that tax policy has a sweeping impact on characteristics regarding their states' competitive composition, which influences economic stability. Population is the key here. Remember, workers are people trying to survive. Survival instincts are practiced by individuals who search for environments which will protect them, and help accomplish their personal financial goals...like a job. The state that captures production will attract greater population.

Think of this growth as growth to the revenue base. When people relocate domestically two things occur...first, they are moving from an economy or community and taking their consumption and their contribution of tax revenue with them. Secondly, they are moving to an area where they will now be contributing revenue to the new state or community economy.

Another example outlined in the *Rich States, Poor States* is the case study *Yankee Doodle Went to...Florida.* This case study illustrates the impact of Connecticut Governor Jodi Rell's decision to enact a 16 percent estate tax. As quoted in their book, "The Wall Street Journal joked that the then Gov. Jeb Bush of Florida should have sent her a thank-you note with a box of chocolate and a ribbon tied around it." Governor Rell and the legislators of Connecticut were hoping the higher taxes would increase tax revenue by $150 million. Not only did the outcome greatly differ from their projections, they also lost an incredible population base, which migrated to Florida.†

Larson's *Stranglehold* cites a case study performed on the city of Philadelphia. In the 1980's, taxes were raised a whopping 19 times, resulting in the city losing 350,000 residents to outlying suburbs. This mass exodus was likely a result of the insane tax burden slapped on the backs of the middle class. Outrageous still, Larson cites a middle class family of four, with earnings of $25,000 paying $3,000 in taxes, the third highest tax burden in the country at the time. Philadelphia paid dearly for these tax increases because the relocation of so many residents unsurprisingly resulted in reduced revenue by diminishing the tax base. What did they do? Taxed 'em again. And again — inflicting more burden on their citizens causing more and more to vacate the city. Despite the poor economic conditions, unions continued muscling their way into city council, demanding "wasteful work rules and less efficient government services." Interestingly, unions were being compensated handsomely. Larson writes, "Government union contracts accounted for over half Philadelphia's budget."

AND...the worst was still to come for Philadelphia, the downtrodden city.

In 1990, a bigger crisis hit the City of Brotherly Love. The city could not sell bonds to finance its debt. Its credit rating plummeted and in January 1991, city operations nearly came to a grinding halt due to a $248 million budget deficit. With help from an outside financial oversight agency and a hefty loan, Philadelphia slowly began to pick up the pieces of a shattered city. It wasn't until the no-nonsense Edward G. Rendell was elected mayor in 1991, that the city began seeing the light at the end of the tunnel. Mayor Rendell went right to work, tackling issues with hard-nosed determination. Larson writes, "He targeted wasteful work rules, sought to privatize certain functions and tried to make government more efficient."

The unions were outraged. How dare this man come in and annihilate all the work they had done? So, unions turned to the only way they knew how to communicate effectively. They initiated a strike. The following excerpt from *Stranglehold* details Mayor Rendell's actions to counteract the unions' intentions.

> *"(Mayor Rendell) activated a strike command center in the Fire Administration Building, which had been stacked with food in case strikers blocked entrances. Two hundred City Hall vehicles were moved to a secret location to thwart union vandals. The city*

switched its radios to a different frequency so they could not be jammed. Non-union employees were ready to take over essential services, such as maintaining water and sewage plants and health centers.

Rendell went on TV to inform the public of the seriousness of the problem and the wastefulness created by union contracts. After just 16 hours, union bosses capitulated. Fed up with high taxes, high crime and filthy streets, Philadelphia rose up to protest the strike and defend their city."

It doesn't get much more American than that...rising up to take back what is theirs; showing the unions that American citizens cannot be bullied or forced to put up with their corrupt practices. Americans need to heed the lessons of Philadelphia and take back what is rightfully ours.

The logic is simple. Higher taxes = lower or lost revenue. This principle is just the tip of the economic iceberg. To further illustrate this point, The Laffer Curve, a tool created by Arthur B. Laffer, a renowned economist offers a clear model representing the impact of tax policy on population migration.

The Laffer Curve begins with the premise that there are two undeniable tax rates that generate zero tax revenue: a zero tax rate and a 100 percent tax rate. Between the two tax rates, zero and 100 percent, the Laffer Curve breaks his model into two ranges; the Normal Range and the Prohibitive Range. As it relates directly to tax revenue; if taxes are raised within the Normal Range, it is thought that tax revenue will increase. However, if taxes are raised to a counterproductive level, within the Prohibitive Range, tax revenue will decrease.

Please see the graph on the next page. Another significant factor regarding where a states' tax rates lie on the Laffer Curve, depends on the tax rates of the neighboring jurisdictions.[†]

Maryland's high cigarette tax is a perfect example of the Laffer Curve in action. Maryland's tax rate was "prohibitive" causing

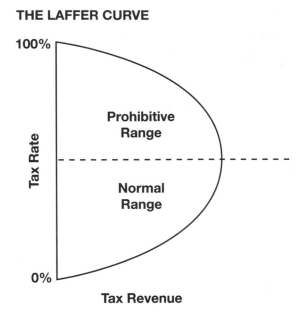

consumption of cigarettes to migrate to neighboring jurisdictions. The net result was lower tax receipts for Maryland while cigarette tax receipts for neighboring states increased.

Even though the Laffer Curve focuses on neighboring jurisdictions and taxes that typically have a high mobility factor, consumption and population migration is becoming more common place—even impacting tax revenues which have historically low mobility (i.e. real estate). We see, in countless examples, that the migration has resulted from businesses, workers and consumers searching for favorable outcomes – lower taxes!

Searching for the threshold and adding principle-based perspectives to lawmakers regarding tax policy, is a critical component to interstate competition. Competition clearly includes the fight for businesses to relocate to their states, job growth opportunities, population migration and favorable tax policy. How do we make our state more attractive? How do we position our state to be the recipient of positive economic migration that contributes to growth?

First, each state must start with a foundation that is conducive to growth. Policy must allow for the evolution of free-market and free-labor. Once a policy such as non-right-to-work laws and high taxation begins to encroach on free markets, economies slow and domestic and global migration begins. What may have appeared as a quick solution becomes the systematic demolition of sound economies. It is the early attraction of the mistletoe and the long-term parasitical decay of competitiveness. If a state does not have the characteristics to compete, it will fail relative to the competition.

What is the fundamental characteristic to compete? Once again, my study demonstrates that right-to-work laws are the key to the foundation contributing to overall manufacturing, corporate, population and consumption migration. Due to the increasing population base, tax revenue in right-to-work states is increasing at a phenomenal pace. Conversely, tax revenues in non-right-to-work states have a negative growth rate, resulting in higher taxes and lower revenue.

While their tax burden is smaller than non-right-to-work states, right-to-work states have seen a net increase in tax revenue growth of over seven percent from 1977 through 2007. The growth in right-to-work states is juxtaposed, with the loss of nearly - 0.5%, during the same time period, for non-right-to-work states.

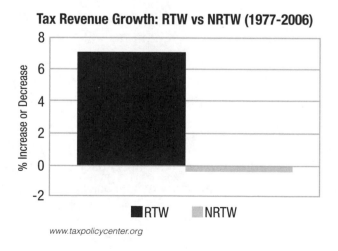

Tax Revenue Growth: RTW vs NRTW (1977-2006)

www.taxpolicycenter.org

The decrease or negative growth in the non-right-to-work state revenue not only threatens the infrastructure of their respective states and the possibility of higher taxes; it can have a negative impact on future investment within the state. Investment, which in many cases, leads to potential new plants, businesses and jobs, that ultimately lead to stability, predictability and more tax revenue.

Housing Starts

Another staggering reality centers on the frequently used "leading" economic indicator – Housing Starts. To establish a basic understanding, an economic indicator is a statistic about the economy. Leading economic indicators, such as housing starts, may act as a barometer of economic performance and forecasts of future performance.

The housing industry accounts for about 27% of investment and capital spending and 5% of the overall United States economy. Sustained *declines* in housing starts will slow the economy, and may push the economy into a recession. *Increases* in housing starts historically triggers economic growth.

The following chart demonstrates yet another trait and more statistical data, to support the compelling arguments that right-to-work states foster economic growth. The migratory impact on housing starts is polarizing. Right-to-work states have experienced 62.46% growth in Housing Units Authorized, while non-right-to-work states have experienced a withering contraction of -6.55%. The difference is 69% in favor of right-to-work. The purpose of building compelling arguments is not to destroy or distort the rights or influences of unions. However, my goal is to build compelling and empirical arguments to protect American jobs and build a sustainable economy. Americans must understand that their choices have an impact...whether short term or long term. The question must always be asked, is there a Mistletoe Effect?

% Change in Housing Units Authorized - RTW vs NRTW

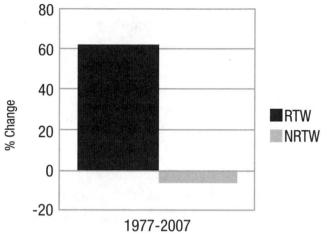

US Census Bureau

We have covered the fact that right-to-work states have a business friendly climate and are considered a more fertile place for profitable business growth. There is less risk knowing that the states right-to-work laws, level the playing field between workers and business. Again, this climate is the foundation that attracts consistent growth.

Below is a model demonstrating the consistent evolution within right-to-work states.

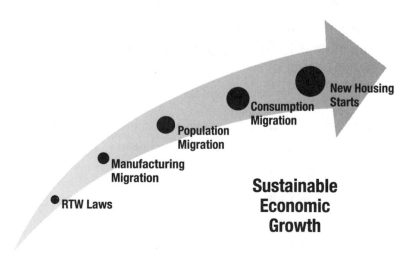

1. **Right-to-Work Laws are the Foundation** – Businesses are looking for a level playing field. Right-to-work laws assist in free-market economics by limiting the impact of outside, unrelated influences such as unions.

2. **Manufacturing Migration** – Right-to-work laws attract manufacturing businesses to their respective states. This occurs due to the fact that right-to-work laws foster free enterprise, supporting worker and employer rights.

3. **Population Migration** – Population migration is a direct result of people, our population, looking to maintain or find work. The general population follows jobs…they follow manufacturing.

4. **Consumption Migration** – Consumption migration directly correlates with population migration. The receiving right-to-work state benefits by the increased population base. The population base, through consumption, begins to organically grow demand which results in higher revenue to the state and the related industries.

5. **New Housing Starts** – This indicator is a demand indicator. Consistently proven over the last 30 years, new housing starts grow faster in right-to-work states. New housing is the pinnacle, winding up right-to-work laws, manufacturing migration, population migration and consumption migration. The increase in population has a direct correlation with the need for homes; basic supply and demand considerations.

6. **Sustainable Economic Growth** – Results from the five above mentioned steps. Housing starts remaining as the culmination and leading economic indicator for growth or recession.

Each state represents a "mini" America. There are two Latin proverbs that come to mind. *"He who standeth with tall trees shall be tall."* The second, *"He that walketh with the lame, shall learn to limp."*

It is very apparent – statistic after statistic and data point after data point; right-to work states are the tall trees. They are growing taller because they embrace the variables and characteristics, which contribute to growth.

Two Shining Examples

Idaho and Texas are two right-to-work states that have recently, enacted Right-to-Work legislation/amendments.

In 1985, Idaho adopted right-to-work status. Before taking action, Idaho had seen a consistent rate of manufacturing jobs LEAVING the state. Between 1977 and 1982, manufacturing jobs were in a steady decline in Idaho, with a 15% drop between those years. Once the right-to-work laws were enacted, manufacturing jobs INCREASED between 1987-2007 by nearly 110%!! Just like that, they more than doubled![†]

Texas is in the same boat, believe-it-or-not. They did not adopt right-to-work laws until 1993. Before 1993, jobs had dropped by over 20%. After their right-to-work laws were enacted, Texas' manufacturing jobs nearly doubled, as did Idaho's.

The underlying factor in all of this is right-to-work status. The economic model stands proven by two states, both of which are seeing the benefits of increased jobs and an increased tax base.

The lame, non-right-to-work states, are struggling to hold on. Their poor choices, as it relates to monetary and fiscal policies, have enlarged the already damaging Mistletoe Effect.

As Americans; federal and state lawmakers, business owners and workers; we need to adopt policy which builds American Industry, American jobs and our global competitiveness. Any time, a self-interested, outside influence undermines the basic necessity of workers keeping their jobs, or businesses operating at a profit...that outside influence must be stopped. After planting the seed for growth...it would be a shame to intentionally remove the lifeblood nourishment we all need to survive...profit.

The Undeniable Truth and Evolution of
Right-to-Work States: 2009

David Williams' 1977 study, demonstrated the economic justification for states to consider and adopt right-to-work laws and initiatives. My 1969-2007 study, reinforces his earlier references, and proves that throughout time, right-to-work laws are beneficial to American workers and American businesses. Below is a powerful summary to reinforce my argument:

Robert S. Graham Foundation Study: 1969 – 2007:
Right to Work (RTW) Non-Right to Work (NRTW)

• RTW Manufacturing job growth outpaced NRTW states by 32%

• RTW Construction job growth outpaced NRTW states by 67%

• RTW Non-Farm job growth outpaced NRTW states by 92%

• RTW Weekly earning growth of manufacturing workers outpaced NRTW states by 6%

• RTW Per-capita income outpaced NRTW states by 10%

• RTW New Housing Units Authorized outpaced NRTW states by 69%

• RTW Capital Expenditures for Manufacturing outpaced NRTW states by 232%

• RTW Tax Revenue Growth outpaced NRTW states by 7.5%

All in all, it is very clear that right-to-work laws increase jobs, sustainability, growth, income for workers, per capita income for the states citizens, increase tax revenue to support the growth of states and business in America. Free America was built on the premise that freedom is our unalienable right. Right-to-work should be considered the *right*…to work.

Below is a study I commissioned through the Robert S. Graham foundation.

The Truth About Right-to-Work

Citizen's Advantage:
The Nuts and Bolts of the Benefits of Right-to-Work

Manufacturing Employment	1977	2007	Actual	Gain %	Difference
-RTW States Average	192,630	247,050	54,420	28%	32%
-NRTW States Average	337,310	324,100	-13,220	-4%	
Construction Employment	1969	2007	Actual	Gain %	Difference
-RTW States Average	72,043.23	247,054.18	175,011.00	268%	67%
-NRTW States Average	102,330.39	324,096.18	221,765.79	201%	
Non-Agricultural Employment	1969	2007	Actual	Gain %	Difference
-RTW States Average	1,224,457.09	2,629,776.82	1,405,319.73	126%	92%
-NRTW States Average	2,134,964.86	2,610,992.46	476,027.61	34%	
Weekly Earnings of Manufacturing Workers	1969	2007	Actual	Gain %	Difference
-RTW States Average	$104.32	$654.05	$549.73	535%	6%
-NRTW States Average	$116.56	$724.36	$607.80	529%	
Per Capita Personal Income	1969	2007	Actual	Gain %	Difference
-RTW States Average	$8,335.64	$19,220.45	$10,884.82	132%	10%
-NRTW States Average	$9,912.39	$21,982.82	$12,070.43	122%	
New Housing Units Authorized	1970	2007	Actual	Gain %	Difference
-RTW States Average	24,702.73	35,544.09	10,841.36	62.46%	69%
-NRTW States Average	29,866.46	21,302.57	-8,563.89	-6.55%	
Capital Expenditures – Manufacturing	1967	2004	Actual	Gain %	Difference
-RTW States Average	$288,440,000	$2,014,040,000	$1,726,000,000	598%	232%
-NRTW States Average	$537,540,000	$2,502,550,000	$1,965,000,000	366%	

US Census Bureau

Collectively, the statistical research demonstrated in the above mentioned charts shows, time and again, states who support and practice right to work laws are better off for a number of reasons,which I've boiled down to the nuts and bolts:

1. Right-to-work laws attract businesses (captial and manufacturing).

2. Businesses attract population (workers searching for and following employment opportunities).

3. Population increase leads to an increase in consumption and the contribution to the tax base.

4. As the tax base and consumption increases, tax revenue increases.

5. As tax revenue increases, lawmakers find themselves in a position to lower or reduce the tax burden placed upon their constitutients. This step will accelarate growth and prosperity.

The converse is easily corrected as well:

1. Non-right-to-work states are not business and investment friendly. In fact, businesses migrate *away* from these states, repelling the opportunity for growth.

2. Negative Business Migration reduces available jobs and encourages people to leave the state.

3. As population decreases, a decrease in consumption and a decrease in contributing tax bases occur. *People follow the jobs to right-to-work states.*

4. As the tax base and consumption decreases, tax revenue to the state decreases.

5. As tax revenue decreases, lawmakers inevitably raise taxes, an attempt to maintain infrastructure, thereby taxing themselves into bigger, deeper holes.

As recently, as October 2009, I drove through my home state of Michigan and my heart wept. I witnessed a once proud and economically viable state wither around a failing automotive industry and out-of-control, escalating taxes. In Detroit, I drove past office buildings once brimming with energy; now boarded up or burned out with workers living in tents on abandoned building's front lawns. Michigan a non-right-to-work state, is a perfect example of tax policy and current organized labor promises, which have leeched the life-giving resources from the industry, loyal people and a willing workforce. This has to stop…

In order to build American jobs, workers can no longer be fooled and our elected officials must not compromise clear benefits to our states. We must protect American jobs! We must protect our nation's ability to manufacture goods and services and remain globally competitive. And we must build a strong foundation for innovation, growth and financial reward to the American worker and the American business.

Forcing someone to adopt, accept or support another's political, and or moral perspective, is wrong and it is fundamentally against the grain of the United States Constitution. Equally against the grain of the U.S. Constitution, would be eliminating a worker's ability to organize, or join a union.

It is very important to stress that our national interests should be focused on maintaining our freedom, human rights, civil liberties increasing our global economic foothold. The historical economic prosperity of the United States of America has benefited the world. We must hang on to the principles that have built this great nation and reclaim our ability to achieve success by doing something about it!

† See appendix for reference.

"All that is necessary for evil to triumph is for good men to do nothing."

— Edmund Burke

CHAPTER TWELVE

Digging Out of Decay

Returning to the
Value of Accomplishment

A t the time of this publication, the national unemployment rate hovers around 10% and is expected to get worse before improving. It is clear the current administration is not doing enough. They enacted policies which are a detriment to our ailing economy.

We must do something to change this pattern. Something productive and strategic. We must make our country more business-friendly and competitive. We need to take the pressure off of free America. Self-imposed, cannibalistic policies such as Non-Right-to-Work (NRTW) laws must be eliminated.

It is clear labor unions in America are undermining our country's ability to thrive and prosper as a free enterprise America — something we simply cannot afford during these dire economic times. As Americans, we need to take back what is ours, rise above the unions, and protect our *right-to-work*. It is time to dig ourselves out of decay.

I have formulated principle-based guidelines to help American government, industry and the American worker find, develop and maintain the global economic advantage.

Finding and Building the American Dream:
State and National Prosperity

We must foster right-to-work laws in all states, promote manufacturing, practice transparency in the workplace, promote and encourage a competitive tax policy and endorse the concept of "buying American." Then, and only then, will our country return to the age of innovation and reward, stabilize and prosper in a free, competitive market.

Right-to-Work

As I've demonstrated through research studies and countless examples, fostering American's right-to-work is the first step in *Finding and Building the American Dream: State and National Prosperity*. Enacting more right-to-work protection in states is the foundation for rebuilding our country. The basic tenant of right-to-work is human rights! It gives workers the ability to choose what they feel is added value to their circumstances. Right-to-work laws bring unions into the free market and constitutionally support their ability to organize in the same free market, without using compulsory means. Citizens, union members, business owners, lawmakers and other elected officials must recognize that "freedom" is best for America. Right-to-work is the new foundation for sustainable economic development.

As we've seen, businesses are attracted to business friendly right-to-work environments. And when businesses relocate to those environments, good things happen to the states that welcome them: increased tax base (population growth), consumption of state and local goods and services and tax revenue growth.

Right-to-work policies take pressure off industry and when industry has room to breathe, profits increase, growth occurs, income for workers increases, consumption grows, tax revenues rise and the cycle repeats itself.

Manufacturing

According to a special report on Forbes.com, 12 million American adults earn a living from manufacturing in the United States and their output accounts for $1.6 trillion—one-fifth of worlds manufacturing. This is more than any other nation, yet domestic manufacturing wallows in a state of crisis. The 12 million American jobs used to be 19.5 million. Manufacturing reached its' peak in 1979 and has fallen every year since.[†]

Through crippling taxation, burdens from labor unions and a difficult work environment, America has made herself vulnerable to her international competitors such as China and India. As we plummet deeper and deeper into the recession, these cuts to America's manufacturing workforce become harder and harder to overcome.

No doubt the landscape of the manufacturing industry in our country has changed. But the concepts remain the same. We need to fertilize the manufacturing industry with investment and innovation in order for it to grow.

One concept to remember is the Profitability Principle. Managers of manufacturing businesses have a fiduciary responsibility to maintain a profitable, not just a viable organization. To oversimplify the model, this means managers must have more revenue then expenses to generate profits.

Revenue – Expenses = Profit or (Loss)

This simple principle is often forgotten. Looking inward, businesses have many variables which influence the expense side of the equation. This reality lends itself to the employers/ businesses searching to find the most "predictable" business environment. Predictable in the sense they are searching for opportunities to operate within a free market, without any sustained, exogenous shock from a third party influence. Outside influences such as labor unions, hostile tax policy, "big" government regulations, etc. limit or greatly reduce predictability relating to expenses. Higher expenses mean lower profitability. In some cases, businesses will raise the prices of their goods and services, which greatly reduces their competitiveness in an ever-encroaching global market.

Having the opportunity to grow manufacturing within a state and our nation, at a fair and reasonable cost, will attract foreign direct investment in manufacturing. It will also increase our nation's ability to export goods and services. Remember, there are many different types of manufacturing: energy, food and beverage, metalworking and telecommunications—just to name a few. Ninety-five percent of the world's consumption takes place outside of the United States. To develop the U.S. economy and that of individual state's—the economy must grow exports. Bringing the world's consumers to the United States' marketplace will accelerate job growth, wealth accumulation for Americans, opportunities and national sovereignty. This is not a national pride, self-indulging statement…it is the reality to survive as an economic world power.

We need to get our fellow Americans out of the unemployment line and back on the assembly line.

Competitive Tax Policy

Since when did we get in the habit of taxing businesses right out of business? I simply cannot fathom why our current administration and many of those in years past, fall into a rut of thinking America's small businesses need to be taxed to death – punished for making a-go-of-it in a free-market economy.

I join millions of Americans who are worried about the Obama administration's current tax proposals. The proposals will limit deferrals on foreign earnings and restrict tax credits on foreign goods – essentially, a tax increase. I think it's fair to say, the last thing Americans need right now is a tax increase of any kind.

This type of policy is the cannibalization of American industry. Business succeeds by the Profitability Principle. If a business cannot operate at a profit, it will have to change its model or ultimately fail. A viable and sustainable business that supports innovation, creativity and commits to research and development ultimately will lead to meeting market demands. The migration of American businesses overseas is a direct result of the destructive, government-imposed policy that destroys the glue that holds the country together.

It is time to cultivate and nurture the aspects of our country which contribute to real economic growth. If a national government must intentionally cannibalize its life-giving "hope" (American industry and its workers) for growth, the government should be forced to change its model. Printing and borrowing money from other nations is a recipe for disaster. Looking inward; increasing taxes for operating revenue and shuffling money stifles opportunity, prosperity and growth. Raising taxes embeds the virus, which slowly kills its host—the *mistletoe effect.* It raises the cost of doing business and blunts our ability to compete globally.

We, as a nation, must recognize the trend lower global tax rates are creating for new businesses, business migration – and economic growth.[†]

Once again, decisions will be made based on the *Profitability Principle.* Today, the United States top corporate tax rates are 35%. Another way to look at this figure is that American based businesses must have 30+% more revenue to even begin to compete at a global level. This hurdle is placed directly in the path of American businesses by their own government. Yet another way to look at it, American-based business may have to raise the cost of

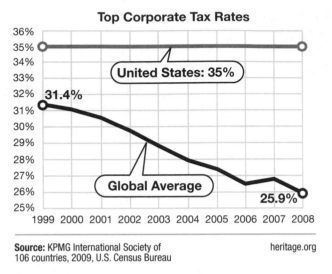

Top Corporate Tax Rates

United States: 35%

31.4%

Global Average

25.9%

1999 2000 2001 2002 2003 2004 2005 2006 2007 2008

Source: KPMG International Society of
106 countries, 2009, U.S. Census Bureau

heritage.org

their products/goods/services by 30+% just to break even with their global counterparts. Regardless – consumers, businesses and the American workers lose.

Rhetoric often blames business migration on The North American Free Trade Agreement (NAFTA) and other similar regulations. The plain truth is this is merely an *excuse* not a *cause*. The quicker we realize we live in a global market, quit making excuses and get into the game...the better off this country will be.

Do not use higher taxes, as a revenue-based solution, to dig out of budget doldrums or to fund bloated government; *incent* with tax policy. To *incent* means bring people and business to the state or our nation by implementing lower tax rates. Attractive, lower tax rates will *incent* companies, or foreign direct investment, to the lower costs of doing business. Taxes unhinge competitive opportunities. Our goal as a nation should be to reward accomplishment and productive risk-taking. By no means should we destroy the incentive to innovate, create and provide. America's industry has led the world into the new millennium. Lawmakers and elected officials must come to the table with real solutions to build America not cannibalize her ability to survive.

Institute Synergistic Workplaces

If there's one thing I've learned in my years as a profitable business owner, it's the importance of synergy in the workplace. A healthy work environment is vital to enjoying a successful, productive workplace where all parties work toward a common goal. Synergy between manager and worker is the key to achievement. Embracing synergy requires transparency – open, honest communication. Managers, take note: the key to productivity and results-driven employees, is transparency. Open the lines of communication. Get real. Get out of your office or out of your cubicle—sit face-to-face with your workers. Educate. Once employees truly grasp what it takes to make the company profitable, and how they will benefit, you will notice a happier, more competent and productive workforce—I guarantee it!

Made in America – Buy American!

Our slogan, "Buy American," often only heard within the United States, should be cast out, like a fishing lure, to the rest of the world. We need to bring world consumption to our country. We've all heard about how we should "Buy American," but few of us truly understand all it involves. Flip over a child's toy and you'll see the standard, "Made in China" or lift up the label on your favorite sweater and you'll see similar wording – "Made in Malaysia". America has become a consumer nation. We are buying the world's goods and they are not buying ours. Why? Cost! American goods are too expensive for middle-class consumers. And how can they not be when our country's marketplace is drenched in unnecessary regulations, over-reacting taxes, parasistic labor unions and limited free markets? Labor unions greatly contribute to this problem by forcing businesses to comply with often ridiculous rules that heavily encroach in company profits. Cost! More Cost! How do we bring global consumption to the United States marketplace?

Texas is one example of a state that has figured out how to bring a piece, a $168 billion dollar piece, of the world's consumption to its' state:

> *"...Texas is a right-to-work state and has been adding jobs by the tens of thousands. Nearly 1,000 new plants have been built in Texas since 2005, from the likes of Microsoft, Samsung and Fujitsu. Foreign-owned companies supplied the state with 345,000 jobs. No wonder Texans don't fear global competition the way some Presidential candidates do."[†]*

Leading the pack with total exports, Texas has built a sustainable economic infrastructure, which has lead to manufacturing migration, corporate and business migration to their state...the world is buying from Texas. This infrastructure, the increased revenue and increase in businesses to their state, has offered a fertile foundation for manufacturing jobs, distribution jobs, corporate and other related jobs growth. To grow our economy we must put Americans to work. Texas is building their state and Texas is supporting American industry.

The following chart illustrates the Top 10 States with respect to their growth in exports. Number 1, Nevada, has had the most growth in exports from 1990 – 2008. It is important to point out that seven out of the top ten states with the most significant growth in state origin exports are right-to-work states.

State	Ranking	Labor Classification	% of Export Growth
Nevada	1	RTW	10.91
Dist of Columbia	2	NRTW	8.52
South Dakota	3	RTW	6.76
Utah	4	RTW	6.21
Nebraska	5	RTW	6.11
Kansas	6	RTW	5.30
Tennessee	7	RTW	5.20
Kentucky	8	NRTW	5.19
South Carolina	9	RTW	5.13
Minnesota	10	NRTW	5.10

U.S. Census Bureau

Conversely, the chart below illustrates the 10 worst states with respect to their growth in exports. Number 50, Rhode Island, has had the lowest growth in exports (1990 – 2008) of all the states in the nation. It is equally important to point out the worst seven out of ten states, regarding growth in state origin exports, are non-right-to-work states.

State	Ranking	Labor Classification	% of Export Growth
Mississippi	41	RTW	2.87
Iowa	42	RTW	2.63
Ohio	43	NRTW	2.61
Delaware	44	NRTW	2.53
Michigan	45	NRTW	2.49
Hawaii	46	NRTW	2.43
Oklahoma	47	RTW	2.42
Maryland	48	NRTW	2.41
Massachusetts	49	NRTW	2.14
Rhode Island	50	NRTW	2.07

U.S. Census Bureau

Fundamentals to consider when reviewing your state or our nation's economic recovery strategies:

1. **Right-to-work laws** – Are we favoring a free enterprise capital market system for employees and their employer? Give freedom to the worker and the employer. Compulsory unionism must end.
2. **Manufacturing** – Are we developing or growing manufacturing within our state or nation?
3. **Taxes** – Are we limiting the capacity for American business growth within our state or nation with a costly and restrictive tax policy?
4. **Jobs for American workers** – Are we expanding our size and quality of our job base within our state or nation? Working Americans are *contributing* Americans.

To untangle the years of neglect and decay, it is going to take time to re-establish a fertile foundation for viable and sustainable growth. Reform and restoration should be words commonly used when discussing the establishment of American business', and the American workers' ability to compete in a global marketplace. Neglecting this vicious cycle endangers society and puts hard working Americans out-of-work.

In addition to contributing to our national economic growth, we must be aware of buying American—we must encourage other countries to-do-so as well. We need attractive goods and services made on U.S. soil. The rest of the world will be inclined to buy American also, improving our national income—bringing jobs, opportunity, prosperity and safety to Americans.

Through the Robert S. Graham Foundation, I will be working with institutes, foundations and organizations across our great nation, to maintain and protect the simple liberties that have nurtured our country to greatness. The foundation will urge education supporting entrepreneurialism and time tested Jeffersonian principles of capitalism and free-market economics. Education will prove to be the foundation for the American citizen to reclaim the American Dream.

† See appendix for reference.

"In defense of the American Dream, we must work together to restore the passion, creativity, innovation and value of accomplishment that built this great nation."
— Robert S. Graham

CHAPTER THIRTEEN

Taking Back the Dream

The Right to Achieve

A merican industry is at a cross-road. Labor unions and the ridiculous regulations imposed on our workforce are keeping us from our right-to-work and distracting us from the American Dream. Historically, Americans thrive under adversity – it is what makes us one of the most powerful nations in the world—we are quickly losing that status. With outside influences tugging at our morals and liberties, Americans need to be steadfast in pursing their American Dream.

In 2007, Forbes.com issued a piece about the American Dream and its various modern-day interpretations. In it, they interviewed well-known political figures, celebrities, academics and sports stars about what the American Dream is to them.

Buzz Aldrin knows a thing or two about achieving the American Dream and is troubled by the direction the "new" American Dream has taken. Aldrin was a pilot on the Apollo 11 moon mission and the second man on the moon in 1969. In his interview with Forbes.com, Aldrin said, "I think the American Dream used to be about achieving one's goals in your field of choice – and from that all other things would follow. Now, I think the dream has morphed into the pursuit of money—accumulate enough of it and the rest will follow. We've become more materialistic. For balance, I think we need to get back to idealism and patriotism, but also be realistic with our monetary goals. I still say, shoot for the moon; you might get there."

Yes, the current economic landscape is dire, but it's not insurmountable. Our country has weathered far worse and not only have we survived adversity—we've thrived as a nation. Even through our country's darkest days, Americans have risen up, taken back what is ours and fought to protect our freedoms and ideals. It's what makes us uniquely American.

Instead of a reversal of the American Dream, we need to treat this reversal like an obstacle, a setback. Americans are fortunate to have the God-given *potential* and in the *right* to achieve the American Dream. We are capable of earning it; it is not handed to us and nor should it be. Truslow Adams was clever with this basic, underlying observation of the American Dream writing: "If the American Dream is to come true and to abide with us, it will, at bottom, depend on the people themselves. If we are able to achieve a richer and fuller life for all, they have got to know what such an achievement implies.[†]

The time has come to refocus and return to the basics of what the American Dream is and what it takes to get there. We need to rekindle that "burn in your belly" passion for our country's way of life. Let us be reborn and start anew. We must take back what is our God-given *right*…the right-to-work under our own freewill, without intimidation or pretenses. We need to celebrate diversity, inspire innovation and drive capitalism. Allow industry to do what it does best – and allow the American worker to prosper.

In 1961, President John F. Kennedy's address to the nation about the importance of space exploration, highlighted the American pride and stamina we need to be reminded of today. He said, "We choose to go to the moon in this decade and other things – not because they are easy, but because they are hard, because that goal will serve to organize and measure the best of our energies and skills, because that challenge is one that we are willing to accept, one we are unwilling to postpone and one which we intend to win."

Part of the essence of having achieved the goal, was the sweat and hard work it took for us to get there—the journey, the sacrifice. WE MUST ACT AND ACT NOW. The real tragedy would be if we remain dormant on these issues and do nothing at all. We must return to the value of accomplishment, let go of the pipedreams and get real. We need to put stock in our abilities and talent—make success happen for ourselves. Then and only then, will we truly get back on track to the American Dream.

"When performance is measured, performance improves. When performance is measured and reported back, the rate of improvement accelerates."

– Thomas S. Monson

CHAPTER FOURTEEN

State Comparison
and Ranking

*Right-to-Work State is Critical
for Economic Growth*

Throughout *Job Killers,* I have made a distinct and statistically supported argument that public policy creating a right-to-work state is critical for economic growth. True economic growth is not a shell game or transfer of wealth from one U.S. citizen to the next. Economic growth means adding to the whole. As a nation, we must attract foreign direct investments and *incent* the global market place to buy American goods and services. Economic growth means more jobs, more opportunity, security and prosperity for Americans.

In an effort to further define the economic advantages created by right-to-work legislation, the following charts, will illustrate the very real advantage right-to-work-states have in comparison to their non-right-to-work neighbors.

To further illustrate pro-growth public policy surrounding labor, I have ranked each state on 8 key dynamic growth factors – how each state ranks within each factor, as-well-as an overall ranking, weighting each state equally.

1) Labor Classification
2) Manufacturing Job Growth
3) Construction Job Growth
4) Non-agricultural Job Growth
5) Per Capita Income Growth
6) New Housing Starts Growth
7) Manufacturing Capital Expenditure Growth
8) State Origin Export Growth

The simple truth…states, their citizens and the workers are being rewarded for pro-growth labor policy. Of the top ten states, nine are right-to-work states. Of the top 25 states, 18 are right-to-work states.

Top 10 States Overall

Dynamic Growth Factors
(9 Right-to-Work States – 1 Non-Right-to-Work state)

State	Labor Classification	Ranking
Nevada	Right-to-Work	1
New Mexico	Non-Right-to-Work	2
Wyoming	Right-to-Work	3
Oklahoma	Right-to-Work Constitutionally based	4
South Dakota	Right-to-Work	5
Utah	Right-to-Work	6
Idaho	Right-to-Work	7
Arizona	Right-to-Work Constitutionally based	8
North Dakota	Right-to-Work	9
North Carolina	Right-to-Work	10

U.S. Census Bureau; Census of Manufacturers

Top 25 States Overall

Dynamic Growth Factors
(18 Right-to-Work States – 7 Non-right-to-Work States)

State	Labor Classification	Ranking
Nevada	Right-to-Work	1
New Mexico	Non-Right-to-Work	2
Wyoming	Right-to-Work	3
Oklahoma	Right-to-Work Constitutionally based	4
South Dakota	Right-to-Work	5
Utah	Right-to-Work	6
Idaho	Right-to-Work	7
Arizona	Right-to-Work Constitutionally based	8
North Dakota	Right-to-Work	9
North Carolina	Right-to-Work	10
Colorado	Non-Right-to-Work	11
Minnesota	Non-Right-to-Work	12
Tennessee	Right-to-Work	13
Texas	Right-to-Work	14
Georgia	Right-to-Work	15
Arkansas	Right-to-Work Constitutionally based	16
Kansas	Right-to-Work	17
Wisconsin	Non-Right-to-Work	18
Oregon	Non-Right-to-Work	19
Florida	Right-to-Work Constitutionally based	20
Washington	Non-Right-to-Work	21
South Carolina	Right-to-Work	22
Alabama	Right-to-Work	23
Nebraska	Right-to-Work	24
New Hampshire	Non-Right-to-Work	25

U.S. Census Bureau; Census of Manufacturers

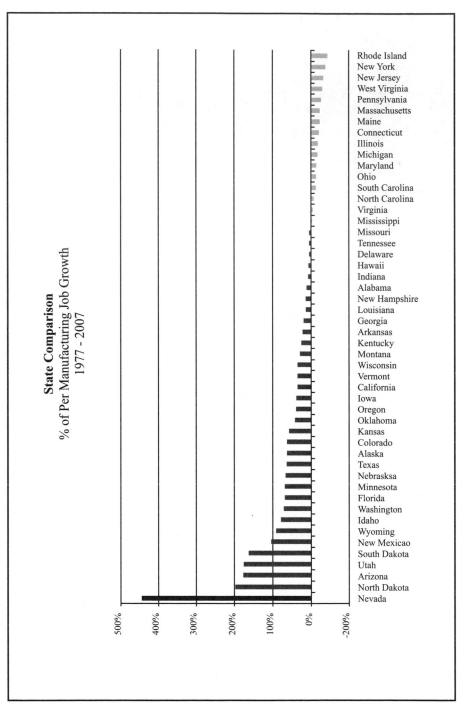

US Census Bureau

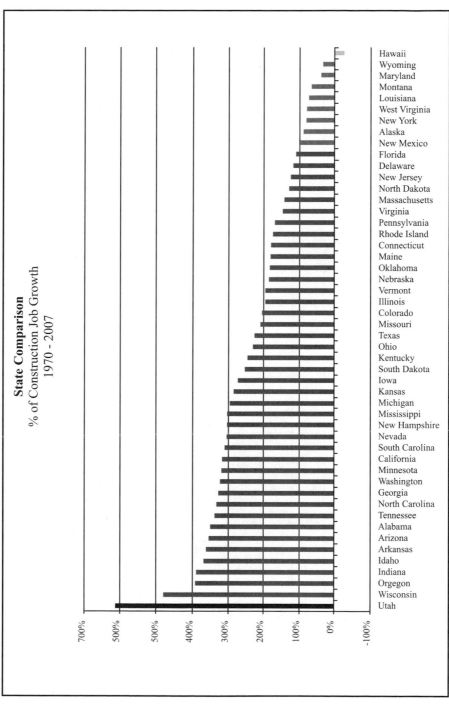

State Comparison
% of Construction Job Growth
1970 - 2007

US Census Bureau

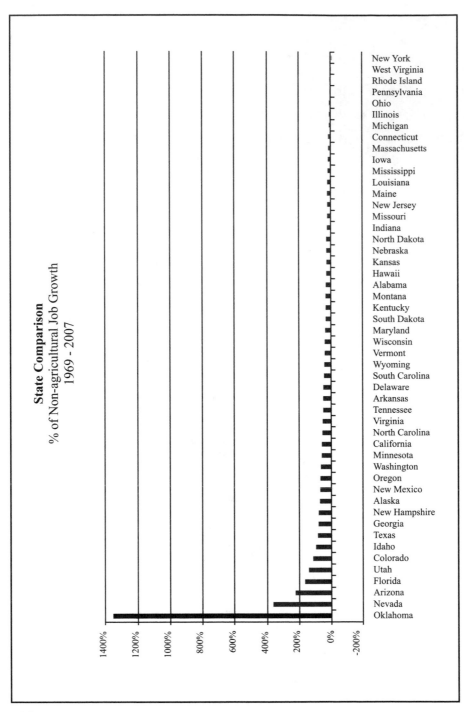

State Comparison
% of Non-agricultural Job Growth
1969 - 2007

New York
West Virginia
Rhode Island
Pennsylvania
Ohio
Illinois
Michigan
Connecticut
Massachusetts
Iowa
Mississippi
Louisiana
Maine
New Jersey
Missouri
Indiana
North Dakota
Nebraska
Kansas
Hawaii
Alabama
Montana
Kentucky
South Dakota
Maryland
Wisconsin
Vermont
Wyoming
South Carolina
Delaware
Arkansas
Tennessee
Virginia
North Carolina
California
Minnesota
Washington
Oregon
New Mexico
Alaska
New Hampshire
Georgia
Texas
Idaho
Colorado
Utah
Florida
Arizona
Nevada
Oklahoma

US Census Bureau

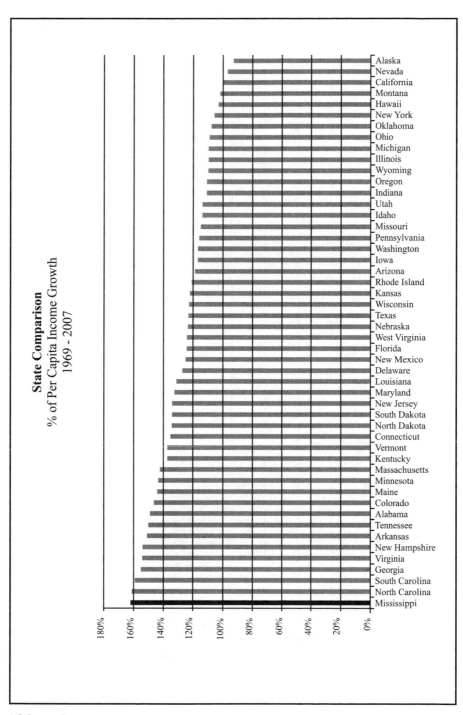

State Comparison
% of Per Capita Income Growth
1969 - 2007

US Census Bureau

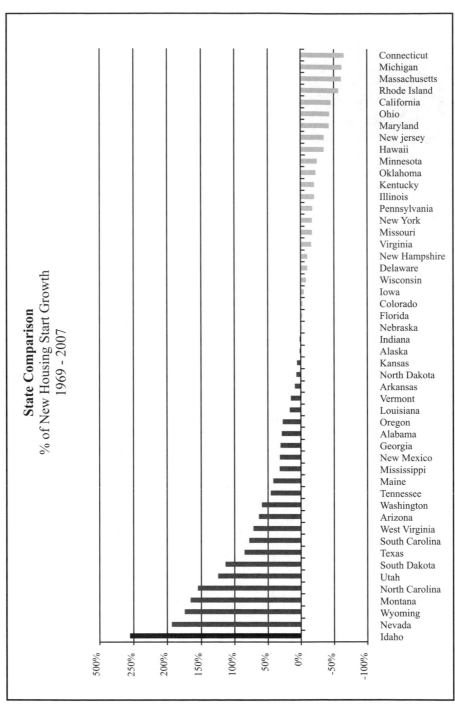

State Comparison
% of New Housing Start Growth
1969 - 2007

US Census Bureau

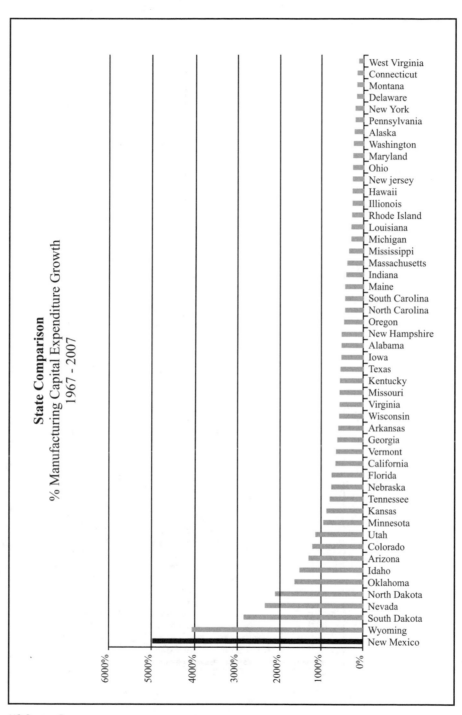

State Comparison
% Manufacturing Capital Expenditure Growth
1967 - 2007

West Virginia
Connecticut
Montana
Delaware
New York
Pennsylvania
Alaska
Washington
Maryland
Ohio
New jersey
Hawaii
Illionois
Rhode Island
Louisiana
Michigan
Mississippi
Massachusetts
Indiana
Maine
South Carolina
North Carolina
Oregon
New Hampshire
Alabama
Iowa
Texas
Kentucky
Missouri
Virginia
Wisconsin
Arkansas
Georgia
Vermont
California
Florida
Nebraska
Tennessee
Kansas
Minnesota
Utah
Colorado
Arizona
Idaho
Oklahoma
North Dakota
Nevada
South Dakota
Wyoming
New Mexico

6000% 5000% 4000% 3000% 2000% 1000% 0%

US Census Bureau

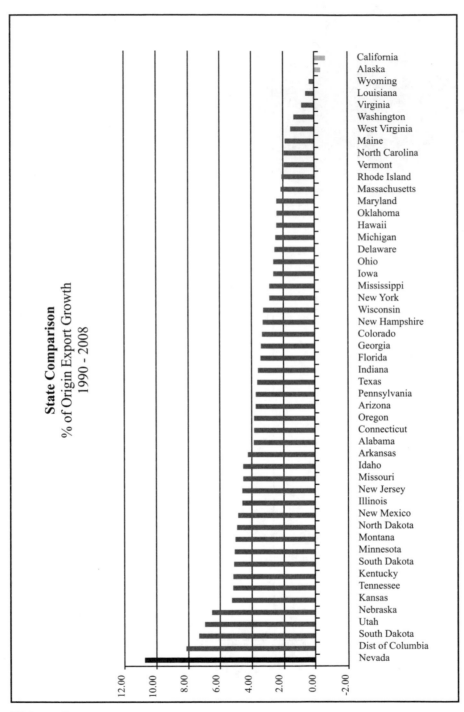

US Census Bureau

"Nothing changes your opinion of a friend so surely as success — yours or his."

– Franklin P. Jones
Saturday Evening Post
November 29, 1953

CHAPTER FIFTEEN

State of the States

Dynamic Growth Factor Performance Ranking
(1=best 50=worst)

A s a nation we must rise up, unify and fight for principles, which support economic growth. With real economic growth, our states and nation will create opportunities, prosperity and security for its' people.

Competition is healthy and offers distinction between success and failures. State of States, this chapter, lines up each of the United States side by side comparing economic growth and state ranking.

The winners are the "Tall Trees" with policy and an environment for lasting economic growth. Our nation should learn by example. Our nation must adopt policy to rebuild the American economy.

*Labor classification is ranked and scored based upon its classification. I have broken the labor classification into three defined classifications with its respective score. 1) Non-Right-to-Work (equals 1 in point value), 2) Legislatively based Right-to-Work (equals 2 in point value) and 3) Constitutionally based Right-to-Work (equals 3 in point value). A score of 1 = least/worst and a score of 3 = most/best. Constitutionally based Right-to-Work states receive the highest point value due to the difficulty to influence and modify its classification.

23 Alabama

Dynamic Growth Factor Performance   Rank: 23

Growth Variable	Data	Rank
Labor Classification	2	-
*(1=least/worst, 3=most/best)**		
Manufacturing Job Growth	12%	29
Construction Job Growth	353%	8
Non-agricultural Job Growth	30%	30
Per Capital Income Growth	149%	9
Housing Starts Growth	29%	18
Manufacturing Capital Expenditures	542%	26
State Origin Export Growth	3.86%	19

36 Alaska

Dynamic Growth Factor Performance   Rank: 36

Growth Variable	Data	Rank
Labor Classification	1	-
(1=least/worst, 3=most/best)		
Manufacturing Job Growth	63%	14
Construction Job Growth	88%	43
Non-agricultural Job Growth	69%	11
Per Capital Income Growth	93%	50
Housing Starts Growth	2%	25
Manufacturing Capital Expenditures	245%	44
State Origin Export Growth	-0.34%	50

*Labor classification is ranked and scored based upon its classification. I have broken the labor classification into three defined classifications with its respective score. 1) Non-Right-to-Work (equals 1 in point value), 2) Legislatively based Right-to-Work (equals 2 in point value) and 3) Constitutionally based Right-to-Work (equals 3 in point value). A score of 1 = least/worst and a score of 3 = most/best. Constitutionally based Right-to-Work states receive the highest point value due to the difficulty to influence and modify its classification.

8 Arizona

Dynamic Growth Factor Performance   **Rank: 8**

Growth Variable	Data	Rank
Labor Classification	3	-
(1=least/worst, 3=most/best)		
Manufacturing Job Growth	178%	3
Construction Job Growth	356%	7
Non-agricultural Job Growth	223%	3
Per Capital Income Growth	119%	31
Housing Starts Growth	64%	11
Manufacturing Capital Expenditures	1312%	8
State Origin Export Growth	3.77%	22

16 Arkansas

Dynamic Growth Factor Performance   **Rank: 16**

Growth Variable	Data	Rank
Labor Classification	3	-
(1=least/worst, 3=most/best)		
Manufacturing Job Growth	22%	25
Construction Job Growth	364%	6
Non-agricultural Job Growth	48%	20
Per Capital Income Growth	151%	7
Housing Starts Growth	9%	22
Manufacturing Capital Expenditures	612%	19
State Origin Export Growth	4.25%	18

*Labor classification is ranked and scored based upon its classification. I have broken the labor classification into three defined classifications with its respective score. 1) Non-Right-to-Work (equals 1 in point value), 2) Legislatively based Right-to-Work (equals 2 in point value) and 3) Constitutionally based Right-to-Work (equals 3 in point value). A score of 1 = least/worst and a score of 3 = most/best. Constitutionally based Right-to-Work states receive the highest point value due to the difficulty to influence and modify its classification.

32 California

Dynamic Growth Factor Performance   Rank: 32

Growth Variable	Data	Rank
Labor Classification	1	-
(1=least/worst, 3=most/best)		
Manufacturing Job Growth	36%	20
Construction Job Growth	317%	14
Non-agricultural Job Growth	58%	16
Per Capital Income Growth	100%	48
Housing Starts Growth	-46%	46
Manufacturing Capital Expenditures	676%	16
State Origin Export Growth	-0.66%	51

11 Colorado

Dynamic Growth Factor Performance   Rank: 11

Growth Variable	Data	Rank
Labor Classification	1	-
(1=least/worst, 3=most/best)		
Manufacturing Job Growth	63%	15
Construction Job Growth	205%	27
Non-agricultural Job Growth	112%	6
Per Capital Income Growth	146%	10
Housing Starts Growth	-2%	29
Manufacturing Capital Expenditures	1221%	9
State Origin Export Growth	3.34%	28

*Labor classification is ranked and scored based upon its classification. I have broken the labor classification into three defined classifications with its respective score. 1) Non-Right-to-Work (equals 1 in point value), 2) Legislatively based Right-to-Work (equals 2 in point value) and 3) Constitutionally based Right-to-Work (equals 3 in point value). A score of 1 = least/worst and a score of 3 = most/best. Constitutionally based Right-to-Work states receive the highest point value due to the difficulty to influence and modify its classification.

46 Connecticut

Dynamic Growth Factor Performance   Rank: 46

Growth Variable	Data	Rank
Labor Classification	1	-
(1=least/worst, 3=most/best)		
Manufacturing Job Growth	-22%	43
Construction Job Growth	180%	33
Non-agricultural Job Growth	13%	43
Per Capital Income Growth	135%	16
Housing Starts Growth	-66%	50
Manufacturing Capital Expenditures	177%	49
State Origin Export Growth	3.86	20

38 Delaware

Dynamic Growth Factor Performance   Rank: 38

Growth Variable	Data	Rank
Labor Classification	1	-
(1=least/worst, 3=most/best)		
Manufacturing Job Growth	6%	32
Construction Job Growth	117%	40
Non-agricultural Job Growth	48%	21
Per Capital Income Growth	127%	22
Housing Starts Growth	-10%	32
Manufacturing Capital Expenditures	183%	47
State Origin Export Growth	2.53%	35

*Labor classification is ranked and scored based upon its classification. I have broken the labor classification into three defined classifications with its respective score. 1) Non-Right-to-Work (equals 1 in point value), 2) Legislatively based Right-to-Work (equals 2 in point value) and 3) Constitutionally based Right-to-Work (equals 3 in point value). A score of 1 = least/worst and a score of 3 = most/best. Constitutionally based Right-to-Work states receive the highest point value due to the difficulty to influence and modify its classification.

20 Florida

Dynamic Growth Factor Performance   Rank: 20

Growth Variable	Data	Rank
Labor Classification	3	-
(1=least/worst, 3=most/best)		
Manufacturing Job Growth	69%	10
Construction Job Growth	109%	41
Non-agricultural Job Growth	162%	4
Per Capital Income Growth	124%	24
Housing Starts Growth	-2%	28
Manufacturing Capital Expenditures	676%	15
State Origin Export Growth	3.45%	26

15 Georgia

Dynamic Growth Factor Performance   Rank: 15

Growth Variable	Data	Rank
Labor Classification	2	-
(1=least/worst, 3=most/best)		
Manufacturing Job Growth	20%	26
Construction Job Growth	329%	11
Non-agricultural Job Growth	79%	9
Per Capital Income Growth	155%	4
Housing Starts Growth	31%	17
Manufacturing Capital Expenditures	625%	18
State Origin Export Growth	3.40%	27

*Labor classification is ranked and scored based upon its classification. I have broken the labor classification into three defined classifications with its respective score. 1) Non-Right-to-Work (equals 1 in point value), 2) Legislatively based Right-to-Work (equals 2 in point value) and 3) Constitutionally based Right-to-Work (equals 3 in point value). A score of 1 = least/worst and a score of 3 = most/best. Constitutionally based Right-to-Work states receive the highest point value due to the difficulty to influence and modify its classification.

49 Hawaii

Dynamic Growth Factor Performance   **Rank: 49**

Growth Variable	Data	Rank
Labor Classification	1	-
(1=least/worst, 3=most/best)		
Manufacturing Job Growth	7%	31
Construction Job Growth	-27%	50
Non-agricultural Job Growth	28%	31
Per Capital Income Growth	103%	46
Housing Starts Growth	-35%	42
Manufacturing Capital Expenditures	281%	39
State Origin Export Growth	2.43%	37

7 Idaho

Dynamic Growth Factor Performance   **Rank: 7**

Growth Variable	Data	Rank
Labor Classification	2	-
(1=least/worst, 3=most/best)		
Manufacturing Job Growth	79%	8
Construction Job Growth	371%	5
Non-agricultural Job Growth	95%	7
Per Capital Income Growth	114%	36
Housing Starts Growth	256%	1
Manufacturing Capital Expenditures	1541%	7
State Origin Export Growth	4.53%	17

*Labor classification is ranked and scored based upon its classification. I have broken the labor classification into three defined classifications with its respective score. 1) Non-Right-to-Work (equals 1 in point value), 2) Legislatively based Right-to-Work (equals 2 in point value) and 3) Constitutionally based Right-to-Work (equals 3 in point value). A score of 1 = least/worst and a score of 3 = most/best. Constitutionally based Right-to-Work states receive the highest point value due to the difficulty to influence and modify its classification.

40 Illinois

Dynamic Growth Factor Performance   Rank: 40

Growth Variable	Data	Rank
Labor Classification	1	-
(1=least/worst, 3=most/best)		
Manufacturing Job Growth	-19%	42
Construction Job Growth	198%	28
Non-agricultural Job Growth	7%	45
Per Capital Income Growth	110%	41
Housing Starts Growth	-21%	38
Manufacturing Capital Expenditures	290%	38
State Origin Export Growth	4.60%	14

29 Indiana

Dynamic Growth Factor Performance   Rank: 29

Growth Variable	Data	Rank
Labor Classification	1	-
(1=least/worst, 3=most/best)		
Manufacturing Job Growth	8%	30
Construction Job Growth	390%	4
Non-agricultural Job Growth	21%	35
Per Capital Income Growth	111%	38
Housing Starts Growth	2%	26
Manufacturing Capital Expenditures	417%	32
State Origin Export Growth	3.59%	25

*Labor classification is ranked and scored based upon its classification. I have broken the labor classification into three defined classifications with its respective score. 1) Non-Right-to-Work (equals 1 in point value), 2) Legislatively based Right-to-Work (equals 2 in point value) and 3) Constitutionally based Right-to-Work (equals 3 in point value). A score of 1 = least/worst and a score of 3 = most/best. Constitutionally based Right-to-Work states receive the highest point value due to the difficulty to influence and modify its classification.

28 Iowa

Dynamic Growth Factor Performance Rank: 28

Growth Variable	Data	Rank
Labor Classification	2	-
(1=least/worst, 3=most/best)		
Manufacturing Job Growth	39%	19
Construction Job Growth	273%	21
Non-agricultural Job Growth	15%	41
Per Capital Income Growth	117%	32
Housing Starts Growth	-4%	30
Manufacturing Capital Expenditures	550%	25
State Origin Export Growth	2.63%	33

17 Kansas

Dynamic Growth Factor Performance Rank: 17

Growth Variable	Data	Rank
Labor Classification	2	-
(1=least/worst, 3=most/best)		
Manufacturing Job Growth	58%	16
Construction Job Growth	286%	20
Non-agricultural Job Growth	25%	32
Per Capital Income Growth	122%	29
Housing Starts Growth	6%	24
Manufacturing Capital Expenditures	892%	12
State Origin Export Growth	5.30%	6

*Labor classification is ranked and scored based upon its classification. I have broken the labor classification into three defined classifications with its respective score. 1) Non-Right-to-Work (equals 1 in point value), 2) Legislatively based Right-to-Work (equals 2 in point value) and 3) Constitutionally based Right-to-Work (equals 3 in point value). A score of 1 = least/worst and a score of 3 = most/best. Constitutionally based Right-to-Work states receive the highest point value due to the difficulty to influence and modify its classification.

31 Kentucky

Dynamic Growth Factor Performance   Rank: 31

Growth Variable	Data	Rank
Labor Classification	1	-
(1=least/worst, 3=most/best)		
Manufacturing Job Growth	26%	24
Construction Job Growth	247%	23
Non-agricultural Job Growth	31%	28
Per Capital Income Growth	137%	14
Housing Starts Growth	-21%	39
Manufacturing Capital Expenditures	562%	23
State Origin Export Growth	5.19%	8

37 Louisiana

Dynamic Growth Factor Performance   Rank: 37

Growth Variable	Data	Rank
Labor Classification	2	-
(1=least/worst, 3=most/best)		
Manufacturing Job Growth	14%	27
Construction Job Growth	74%	46
Non-agricultural Job Growth	17%	39
Per Capital Income Growth	131%	21
Housing Starts Growth	17%	20
Manufacturing Capital Expenditures	300%	36
State Origin Export Growth	0.58%	48

*Labor classification is ranked and scored based upon its classification. I have broken the labor classification into three defined classifications with its respective score. 1) Non-Right-to-Work (equals 1 in point value), 2) Legislatively based Right-to-Work (equals 2 in point value) and 3) Constitutionally based Right-to-Work (equals 3 in point value). A score of 1 = least/worst and a score of 3 = most/best. Constitutionally based Right-to-Work states receive the highest point value due to the difficulty to influence and modify its classification.

34 Maine

Dynamic Growth Factor Performance **Rank: 34**

Growth Variable	Data	Rank
Labor Classification	1	-
(1=least/worst, 3=most/best)		
Manufacturing Job Growth	-24%	44
Construction Job Growth	182%	32
Non-agricultural Job Growth	19%	38
Per Capital Income Growth	144%	11
Housing Starts Growth	42%	14
Manufacturing Capital Expenditures	447%	31
State Origin Export Growth	1.89%	44

47 Maryland

Dynamic Growth Factor Performance **Rank: 47**

Growth Variable	Data	Rank
Labor Classification	1	-
(1=least/worst, 3=most/best)		
Manufacturing Job Growth	-15%	40
Construction Job Growth	38%	48
Non-agricultural Job Growth	35%	26
Per Capital Income Growth	132%	20
Housing Starts Growth	-43%	44
Manufacturing Capital Expenditures	267%	42
State Origin Export Growth	2.41%	39

*Labor classification is ranked and scored based upon its classification. I have broken the labor classification into three defined classifications with its respective score. 1) Non-Right-to-Work (equals 1 in point value), 2) Legislatively based Right-to-Work (equals 2 in point value) and 3) Constitutionally based Right-to-Work (equals 3 in point value). A score of 1 = least/worst and a score of 3 = most/best. Constitutionally based Right-to-Work states receive the highest point value due to the difficulty to influence and modify its classification.

43 Massachusetts

Dynamic Growth Factor Performance   **Rank: 43**

Growth Variable	Data	Rank
Labor Classification	1	-
(1=least/worst, 3=most/best)		
Manufacturing Job Growth	-24%	45
Construction Job Growth	141%	37
Non-agricultural Job Growth	14%	42
Per Capital Income Growth	142%	13
Housing Starts Growth	-62%	48
Manufacturing Capital Expenditures	404%	33
State Origin Export Growth	2.14%	40

39 Michigan

Dynamic Growth Factor Performance   **Rank: 39**

Growth Variable	Data	Rank
Labor Classification	1	-
(1=least/worst, 3=most/best)		
Manufacturing Job Growth	-18%	41
Construction Job Growth	298%	19
Non-agricultural Job Growth	8%	44
Per Capital Income Growth	110%	42
Housing Starts Growth	-63%	49
Manufacturing Capital Expenditures	310%	36
State Origin Export Growth	2.49%	5

*Labor classification is ranked and scored based upon its classification. I have broken the labor classification into three defined classifications with its respective score. 1) Non-Right-to-Work (equals 1 in point value), 2) Legislatively based Right-to-Work (equals 2 in point value) and 3) Constitutionally based Right-to-Work (equals 3 in point value). A score of 1 = least/worst and a score of 3 = most/best. Constitutionally based Right-to-Work states receive the highest point value due to the difficulty to influence and modify its classification.

12 Minnesota

Dynamic Growth Factor Performance   Rank: 12

Growth Variable	Data	Rank
Labor Classification	1	-
(1=least/worst, 3=most/best)		
Manufacturing Job Growth	69%	11
Construction Job Growth	321%	13
Non-agricultural Job Growth	59%	15
Per Capital Income Growth	143%	12
Housing Starts Growth	-25%	41
Manufacturing Capital Expenditures	961%	11
State Origin Export Growth	5.10%	10

26 Mississippi

Dynamic Growth Factor Performance   Rank: 26

Growth Variable	Data	Rank
Labor Classification	3	-
(1=least/worst, 3=most/best)		
Manufacturing Job Growth	-2%	35
Construction Job Growth	304%	18
Non-agricultural Job Growth	17%	40
Per Capital Income Growth	162%	1
Housing Starts Growth	32%	15
Manufacturing Capital Expenditures	361%	34
State Origin Export Growth	2.87%	32

*Labor classification is ranked and scored based upon its classification. I have broken the labor classification into three defined classifications with its respective score. 1) Non-Right-to-Work (equals 1 in point value), 2) Legislatively based Right-to-Work (equals 2 in point value) and 3) Constitutionally based Right-to-Work (equals 3 in point value). A score of 1 = least/worst and a score of 3 = most/best. Constitutionally based Right-to-Work states receive the highest point value due to the difficulty to influence and modify its classification.

35 Missouri

Dynamic Growth Factor Performance   Rank: 35

Growth Variable	Data	Rank
Labor Classification	1	-
(1=least/worst, 3=most/best)		
Manufacturing Job Growth	5%	34
Construction Job Growth	208%	26
Non-agricultural Job Growth	20%	36
Per Capital Income Growth	115%	35
Housing Starts Growth	-17%	35
Manufacturing Capital Expenditures	578%	22
State Origin Export Growth	4.59%	16

30 Montana

Dynamic Growth Factor Performance   Rank: 30

Growth Variable	Data	Rank
Labor Classification	1	-
(1=least/worst, 3=most/best)		
Manufacturing Job Growth	30%	23
Construction Job Growth	65%	47
Non-agricultural Job Growth	31%	29
Per Capital Income Growth	102%	47
Housing Starts Growth	166%	4
Manufacturing Capital Expenditures	180	48
State Origin Export Growth	5.06%	11

*Labor classification is ranked and scored based upon its classification. I have broken the labor classification into three defined classifications with its respective score. 1) Non-Right-to-Work (equals 1 in point value), 2) Legislatively based Right-to-Work (equals 2 in point value) and 3) Constitutionally based Right-to-Work (equals 3 in point value). A score of 1 = least/worst and a score of 3 = most/best. Constitutionally based Right-to-Work states receive the highest point value due to the difficulty to influence and modify its classification.

24 Nebraska

Dynamic Growth Factor Performance   **Rank: 24**

Growth Variable	Data	Rank
Labor Classification	2	-
(1=least/worst, 3=most/best)		
Manufacturing Job Growth	67%	12
Construction Job Growth	186%	30
Non-agricultural Job Growth	25%	33
Per Capital Income Growth	123%	26
Housing Starts Growth	-1%	27
Manufacturing Capital Expenditures	766%	14
State Origin Export Growth	6.11%	5

1 Nevada

Dynamic Growth Factor Performance   **Rank: 1**

Growth Variable	Data	Rank
Labor Classification	2	-
(1=least/worst, 3=most/best)		
Manufacturing Job Growth	445%	1
Construction Job Growth	305%	16
Non-agricultural Job Growth	363%	2
Per Capital Income Growth	97%	49
Housing Starts Growth	194%	2
Manufacturing Capital Expenditures	2367%	4
State Origin Export Growth	10.91%	1

*Labor classification is ranked and scored based upon its classification. I have broken the labor classification into three defined classifications with its respective score. 1) Non-Right-to-Work (equals 1 in point value), 2) Legislatively based Right-to-Work (equals 2 in point value) and 3) Constitutionally based Right-to-Work (equals 3 in point value). A score of 1 = least/worst and a score of 3 = most/best. Constitutionally based Right-to-Work states receive the highest point value due to the difficulty to influence and modify its classification.

25 New Hampshire

Dynamic Growth Factor Performance   Rank: 25

Growth Variable	Data	Rank
Labor Classification	1	-
(1=least/worst, 3=most/best)		
Manufacturing Job Growth	14%	28
Construction Job Growth	305%	17
Non-agricultural Job Growth	77%	10
Per Capital Income Growth	154%	6
Housing Starts Growth	-10%	33
Manufacturing Capital Expenditures	529%	27
State Origin Export Growth	3.28%	29

45 New Jersey

Dynamic Growth Factor Performance   Rank: 45

Growth Variable	Data	Rank
Labor Classification	1	-
(1=least/worst, 3=most/best)		
Manufacturing Job Growth	-33%	48
Construction Job Growth	124%	39
Non-agricultural Job Growth	20%	37
Per Capital Income Growth	134%	19
Housing Starts Growth	-35%	43
Manufacturing Capital Expenditures	278%	40
State Origin Export Growth	4.59%	15

*Labor classification is ranked and scored based upon its classification. I have broken the labor classification into three defined classifications with its respective score. 1) Non-Right-to-Work (equals 1 in point value), 2) Legislatively based Right-to-Work (equals 2 in point value) and 3) Constitutionally based Right-to-Work (equals 3 in point value). A score of 1 = least/worst and a score of 3 = most/best. Constitutionally based Right-to-Work states receive the highest point value due to the difficulty to influence and modify its classification.

2 New Mexico

Dynamic Growth Factor Performance   Rank: 2

Growth Variable	Data	Rank
Labor Classification	1	-
(1=least/worst, 3=most/best)		
Manufacturing Job Growth	104%	6
Construction Job Growth	98%	42
Non-agricultural Job Growth	68%	12
Per Capital Income Growth	125%	23
Housing Starts Growth	32%	16
Manufacturing Capital Expenditures	4976%	1
State Origin Export Growth	4.86%	13

50 New York

Dynamic Growth Factor Performance   Rank: 50

Growth Variable	Data	Rank
Labor Classification	1	-
(1=least/worst, 3=most/best)		
Manufacturing Job Growth	-39%	49
Construction Job Growth	80%	44
Non-agricultural Job Growth	-11%	50
Per Capital Income Growth	106%	45
Housing Starts Growth	-17%	36
Manufacturing Capital Expenditures	213%	46
State Origin Export Growth	2.87%	31

*Labor classification is ranked and scored based upon its classification. I have broken the labor classification into three defined classifications with its respective score. 1) Non-Right-to-Work (equals 1 in point value), 2) Legislatively based Right-to-Work (equals 2 in point value) and 3) Constitutionally based Right-to-Work (equals 3 in point value). A score of 1 = least/worst and a score of 3 = most/best. Constitutionally based Right-to-Work states receive the highest point value due to the difficulty to influence and modify its classification.

10 North Carolina

Dynamic Growth Factor Performance   **Rank: 10**

Growth Variable	Data	Rank
Labor Classification	2	-
(1=least/worst, 3=most/best)		
Manufacturing Job Growth	-8%	37
Construction Job Growth	334%	10
Non-agricultural Job Growth	55%	17
Per Capital Income Growth	161%	2
Housing Starts Growth	155%	5
Manufacturing Capital Expenditures	450%	29
State Origin Export Growth	2.01%	43

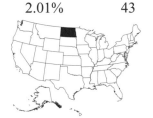

9 North Dakota

Dynamic Growth Factor Performance   **Rank: 9**

Growth Variable	Data	Rank
Labor Classification	2	-
(1=least/worst, 3=most/best)		
Manufacturing Job Growth	198%	2
Construction Job Growth	130%	38
Non-agricultural Job Growth	24%	34
Per Capital Income Growth	134%	17
Housing Starts Growth	7%	23
Manufacturing Capital Expenditures	2119%	5
State Origin Export Growth	4.94%	12

*Labor classification is ranked and scored based upon its classification. I have broken the labor classification into three defined classifications with its respective score. 1) Non-Right-to-Work (equals 1 in point value), 2) Legislatively based Right-to-Work (equals 2 in point value) and 3) Constitutionally based Right-to-Work (equals 3 in point value). A score of 1 = least/worst and a score of 3 = most/best. Constitutionally based Right-to-Work states receive the highest point value due to the difficulty to influence and modify its classification.

42 Ohio

Dynamic Growth Factor Performance   **Rank: 42**

Growth Variable	Data	Rank
Labor Classification	1	-
(1=least/worst, 3=most/best)		
Manufacturing Job Growth	-14%	39
Construction Job Growth	231%	24
Non-agricultural Job Growth	6%	46
Per Capital Income Growth	109%	43
Housing Starts Growth	-44%	45
Manufacturing Capital Expenditures	274%	41
State Origin Export Growth	2.61%	34

4 Oklahoma

Dynamic Growth Factor Performance   **Rank: 4**

Growth Variable	Data	Rank
Labor Classification	3	-
(1=least/worst, 3=most/best)		
Manufacturing Job Growth	43%	17
Construction Job Growth	183%	31
Non-agricultural Job Growth	1146%	1
Per Capital Income Growth	108%	44
Housing Starts Growth	-23%	40
Manufacturing Capital Expenditures	1659%	6
State Origin Export Growth	2.42%	38

*Labor classification is ranked and scored based upon its classification. I have broken the labor classification into three defined classifications with its respective score. 1) Non-Right-to-Work (equals 1 in point value), 2) Legislatively based Right-to-Work (equals 2 in point value) and 3) Constitutionally based Right-to-Work (equals 3 in point value). A score of 1 = least/worst and a score of 3 = most/best. Constitutionally based Right-to-Work states receive the highest point value due to the difficulty to influence and modify its classification.

19 Oregon

Dynamic Growth Factor Performance   Rank: 19

Growth Variable	Data	Rank
Labor Classification	1	-
(1=least/worst, 3=most/best)		
Manufacturing Job Growth	40%	18
Construction Job Growth	393%	3
Non-agricultural Job Growth	68%	13
Per Capital Income Growth	111%	39
Housing Starts Growth	28%	19
Manufacturing Capital Expenditures	465%	28
State Origin Export Growth	3.86%	21

44 Pennsylvania

Dynamic Growth Factor Performance   Rank: 44

Growth Variable	Data	Rank
Labor Classification	1	-
(1=least/worst, 3=most/best)		
Manufacturing Job Growth	-27%	46
Construction Job Growth	171%	35
Non-agricultural Job Growth	1%	47
Per Capital Income Growth	116%	34
Housing Starts Growth	-18%	37
Manufacturing Capital Expenditures	216%	45
State Origin Export Growth	3.75%	23

*Labor classification is ranked and scored based upon its classification. I have broken the labor classification into three defined classifications with its respective score. 1) Non-Right-to-Work (equals 1 in point value), 2) Legislatively based Right-to-Work (equals 2 in point value) and 3) Constitutionally based Right-to-Work (equals 3 in point value). A score of 1 = least/worst and a score of 3 = most/best. Constitutionally based Right-to-Work states receive the highest point value due to the difficulty to influence and modify its classification.

48 Rhode Island

Dynamic Growth Factor Performance   Rank: 48

Growth Variable	Data	Rank
Labor Classification	1	-
(1=least/worst, 3=most/best)		
Manufacturing Job Growth	-44%	50
Construction Job Growth	176%	34
Non-agricultural Job Growth	1%	48
Per Capital Income Growth	121%	30
Housing Starts Growth	-58%	47
Manufacturing Capital Expenditures	293%	37
State Origin Export Growth	2.07%	41

22 South Carolina

Dynamic Growth Factor Performance   Rank: 22

Growth Variable	Data	Rank
Labor Classification	2	-
(1=least/worst, 3=most/best)		
Manufacturing Job Growth	-14%	38
Construction Job Growth	311%	15
Non-agricultural Job Growth	45%	22
Per Capital Income Growth	159%	3
Housing Starts Growth	78%	9
Manufacturing Capital Expenditures	449%	30
State Origin Export Growth	5.13%	9

*Labor classification is ranked and scored based upon its classification. I have broken the labor classification into three defined classifications with its respective score. 1) Non-Right-to-Work (equals 1 in point value), 2) Legislatively based Right-to-Work (equals 2 in point value) and 3) Constitutionally based Right-to-Work (equals 3 in point value). A score of 1 = least/worst and a score of 3 = most/best. Constitutionally based Right-to-Work states receive the highest point value due to the difficulty to influence and modify its classification.

5 South Dakota

Dynamic Growth Factor Performance   Rank: 5

Growth Variable	Data	Rank
Labor Classification	2	-
(1=least/worst, 3=most/best)		
Manufacturing Job Growth	164%	5
Construction Job Growth	255%	22
Non-agricultural Job Growth	33%	27
Per Capital Income Growth	134%	18
Housing Starts Growth	114%	7
Manufacturing Capital Expenditures	2861%	3
State Origin Export Growth	6.76%	3

13 Tennessee

Dynamic Growth Factor Performance   Rank: 13

Growth Variable	Data	Rank
Labor Classification	2	-
(1=least/worst, 3=most/best)		
Manufacturing Job Growth	5%	33
Construction Job Growth	339%	9
Non-agricultural Job Growth	50%	19
Per Capital Income Growth	150%	8
Housing Starts Growth	46%	13
Manufacturing Capital Expenditures	811%	13
State Origin Export Growth	5.20%	7

*Labor classification is ranked and scored based upon its classification. I have broken the labor classification into three defined classifications with its respective score. 1) Non-Right-to-Work (equals 1 in point value), 2) Legislatively based Right-to-Work (equals 2 in point value) and 3) Constitutionally based Right-to-Work (equals 3 in point value). A score of 1 = least/worst and a score of 3 = most/best. Constitutionally based Right-to-Work states receive the highest point value due to the difficulty to influence and modify its classification.

14 Texas

Dynamic Growth Factor Performance   **Rank: 14**

Growth Variable	Data	Rank
Labor Classification	2	-
(1=least/worst, 3=most/best)		
Manufacturing Job Growth	65%	13
Construction Job Growth	227%	25
Non-agricultural Job Growth	83%	8
Per Capital Income Growth	123%	27
Housing Starts Growth	85%	8
Manufacturing Capital Expenditures	559%	24
State Origin Export Growth	3.65%	24

6 Utah

Dynamic Growth Factor Performance   **Rank: 6**

Growth Variable	Data	Rank
Labor Classification	2	-
(1=least/worst, 3=most/best)		
Manufacturing Job Growth	177%	4
Construction Job Growth	615%	1
Non-agricultural Job Growth	140%	5
Per Capital Income Growth	114%	37
Housing Starts Growth	125%	6
Manufacturing Capital Expenditures	1145%	10
State Origin Export Growth	6.21%	4

*Labor classification is ranked and scored based upon its classification. I have broken the labor classification into three defined classifications with its respective score. 1) Non-Right-to-Work (equals 1 in point value), 2) Legislatively based Right-to-Work (equals 2 in point value) and 3) Constitutionally based Right-to-Work (equals 3 in point value). A score of 1 = least/worst and a score of 3 = most/best. Constitutionally based Right-to-Work states receive the highest point value due to the difficulty to influence and modify its classification.

27 Vermont

Dynamic Growth Factor Performance   Rank: 27

Growth Variable	Data	Rank
Labor Classification	1	-
(1=least/worst, 3=most/best)		
Manufacturing Job Growth	36%	21
Construction Job Growth	197%	29
Non-agricultural Job Growth	39%	24
Per Capital Income Growth	137%	15
Housing Starts Growth	15%	21
Manufacturing Capital Expenditures	648%	17
State Origin Export Growth	2.01%	42

33 Virginia

Dynamic Growth Factor Performance   Rank: 33

Growth Variable	Data	Rank
Labor Classification	2	-
(1=least/worst, 3=most/best)		
Manufacturing Job Growth	-4%	36
Construction Job Growth	147%	36
Non-agricultural Job Growth	54%	18
Per Capital Income Growth	154%	5
Housing Starts Growth	-16%	34
Manufacturing Capital Expenditures	580%	21
State Origin Export Growth	0.84%	47

*Labor classification is ranked and scored based upon its classification. I have broken the labor classification into three defined classifications with its respective score. 1) Non-Right-to-Work (equals 1 in point value), 2) Legislatively based Right-to-Work (equals 2 in point value) and 3) Constitutionally based Right-to-Work (equals 3 in point value). A score of 1 = least/worst and a score of 3 = most/best. Constitutionally based Right-to-Work states receive the highest point value due to the difficulty to influence and modify its classification.

21 Washington

Dynamic Growth Factor Performance   **Rank: 21**

Growth Variable	Data	Rank
Labor Classification	1	-
(1=least/worst, 3=most/best)		
Manufacturing Job Growth	72%	9
Construction Job Growth	324%	12
Non-agricultural Job Growth	65%	14
Per Capital Income Growth	117%	33
Housing Starts Growth	59%	12
Manufacturing Capital Expenditures	251%	43
State Origin Export Growth	1.33%	46

41 West Virginia

Dynamic Growth Factor Performance   **Rank: 41**

Growth Variable	Data	Rank
Labor Classification	1	-
(1=least/worst, 3=most/best)		
Manufacturing Job Growth	-31%	47
Construction Job Growth	79%	45
Non-agricultural Job Growth	-6%	49
Per Capital Income Growth	124%	25
Housing Starts Growth	72%	10
Manufacturing Capital Expenditures	131%	50
State Origin Export Growth	1.55%	45

*Labor classification is ranked and scored based upon its classification. I have broken the labor classification into three defined classifications with its respective score. 1) Non-Right-to-Work (equals 1 in point value), 2) Legislatively based Right-to-Work (equals 2 in point value) and 3) Constitutionally based Right-to-Work (equals 3 in point value). A score of 1 = least/worst and a score of 3 = most/best. Constitutionally based Right-to-Work states receive the highest point value due to the difficulty to influence and modify its classification.

18 Wisconsin

Dynamic Growth Factor Performance

Rank: 18

Growth Variable	Data	Rank
Labor Classification	1	-
(1=least/worst, 3=most/best)		
Manufacturing Job Growth	36%	22
Construction Job Growth	478%	2
Non-agricultural Job Growth	38%	25
Per Capital Income Growth	123%	28
Housing Starts Growth	-8%	31
Manufacturing Capital Expenditures	593%	20
State Origin Export Growth	3.26%	30

3 Wyoming

Dynamic Growth Factor Performance

Rank: 3

Growth Variable	Data	Rank
Labor Classification	2	-
(1=least/worst, 3=most/best)		
Manufacturing Job Growth	92%	7
Construction Job Growth	33%	49
Non-agricultural Job Growth	41%	23
Per Capital Income Growth	110%	40
Housing Starts Growth	174%	3
Manufacturing Capital Expenditures	4079%	2
State Origin Export Growth	0.36%	49

*Labor classification is ranked and scored based upon its classification. I have broken the labor classification into three defined classifications with its respective score. 1) Non-Right-to-Work (equals 1 in point value), 2) Legislatively based Right-to-Work (equals 2 in point value) and 3) Constitutionally based Right-to-Work (equals 3 in point value). A score of 1 = least/worst and a score of 3 = most/best. Constitutionally based Right-to-Work states receive the highest point value due to the difficulty to influence and modify its classification.

Robert S. Graham

Robert S. Graham has an outstanding record of leadership and experience in serving Arizona residents and charitable organizations through his commitment of time and financial contributions. Graham is also an accomplished businessman, recognized regionally by AZ Business Magazine as one of the Top Entrepreneurs and nationally, by Boomer Market Advisor magazine as the 2007 Advisor of the Year.

A cum laude graduate from Arizona State University with a Bachelor of Science in Global Business Management and Finance. Graham has served on the ASU School of Global Business Management and Leadership Dean's Advisory Council. For his entrepreneurial success and service to ASU, Graham was awarded "Distinguished Alumnus" from the School of Global Management and Leadership.

Since 1993, Graham has worked with and educated thousands of individuals and organizations ranging from Fortune 500 companies to private clients. Graham has been invited as an expert to present on topics, which include taxations, innovation, entrepreneurialism, globalization, wealth accumulation, capital markets, tax efficiencies, legacy planning, asset protection and business/practice succession. He has assisted small, middle-market, and large corporations in applying easy-to-implement financial engineering, marketing and operating programs to immediately improve short-term results while maintaining long-range investment strategy and continuity.

Graham is President and CEO of RG Capital, responsible for the company's financial advisory, investment banking/consulting and corporate development business. He brings more than twelve years of experience in domestic and international strategic, financial, marketing, corporate development and operational management. Additionally, he has profitably managed three operating companies and three venture start-ups.

Robert Graham has been chosen as a featured presenter for the Financial Advisor Symposium 2005, 2006, 2007 and the Arizona State University Financial Management Association. Graham was also honored in May 2007, giving a motivational convocation to the graduating students at ASU's School of Global Business Leadership and Management.

Graham was recently added to the "Distinguished Speaker Series" of the Haworth College of Business at Western Michigan University in his home state of Michigan. His topic centered on "Globalization" and Michigan's opportunities to become globally competitive, while promoting economic development and sustainability.

In May 2008, Graham received a Presidential Commission and a Reagan Congressional Commission by the National Republican Congressional Committee recognizing Graham's lifelong commitment, contribution and service as a Republican. Graham is a member of the Arizona GOP Leadership council which serves to support and foster leadership, vision and the growth of the Arizona Republican Party...he is also a life member of the National Rifle Association.

Graham has lived in Arizona for sixteen years. He and his wife, Julia, reside in Phoenix with their four children. The Grahams are active members in their church and local community. They also give suport to local and international charities such as: Catholic Charities, New Beginnings Women Shelter, Saint Mary's Food Bank, Habitat for Humanity, Healing Hands for Haiti, among others.

Appendix

Unattainable or Forgotten?

Smith, William. Telephone Interview. 27 July 2009.

"ABOUT THE WHITE HOUSE PRESIDENTS: ABRAHAM LINCOLN." whitehouse.gov. n.d. Web. 30 July 2009.

Adams, James Truslow. *The Epic of America*. 1931. Safety Harbor: Simon Publications, 2001. Print.

Jefferson, Thomas et. al. *Declaration of Independence*. 4 July 1776. Web. 30 September 2009. <http://www.archives.gov/exhibits/charters/declaration.html>

Longley, Robert. "Two Thirds Feel American Dream is Harder to Achieve." about.com. 1 October 2004. Web. 15 September 2009. <http://usgovinfo.about.com/od/moneymatters/a/baddream.htm>.

Bazient, Kenneth and Michael McAuliff. "President Barack Obama Touts Middle-Class Task Force Led By VP Joe Biden." nydailynews.com New York Daily News, 30 January 2009. Web. 10 September 2009. <http://www.nydailynews.com/news/politics/2009/01/30/2009-01-30_president_barack_obama_touts_middleclass.html>

Kamp, David. "Rethinking the American Dream." *Vanity Fair* April 2009: Print.

Sherk, James. "Do Americans Today Still Need Labor Unions?" heritage.org. 1 April 2008. Web. 29 July 2009. <http://www.heritage.org/press/commentary/ed040108c.cfm>

Irvine, Martha. "Young Labeled 'Entitlement Generation'" freerepublic.com. *Associated Press*. 26 June 2005. Web. 1 October 2009. <http://www.freerepublic.com/focus/f-news/1431497/posts>

Twenge, M. Jean, Ph.D. *Generation Me: Why Today's Young Americans are More Confident, Assertive, Entitled – and More Miserable Than Ever Before*. New York: Free Press, 2006. Print.

"LOTTERIES" http://govinfo.library.unt.edu National Gambling Impact Study Commission. n.d. Web. 30 July 2009. <http://govinfo.library.unt.edu/ngisc/research/lotteries.html>

Clotfelter, Charles T. and Philip J. Cook. *Selling Hope* 1989. Cambridge: First Harvard University Press, 1991. Print.

Hagerty, Bob. Telephone Interview. 2 December 2009.

Labor Unions

McCullough, David. *John Adams*. New York: Simon & Schuster, 2001. Print.

Foner, Philip S. *History of the Labor Movement: From Colonial Times to the Founding of the American Federation of Labor*. Seventh printing. New York: International Publishers Co., Inc. 1982. Print.

"THE GILDED AGE." Gilder Lehrman Institute of American History n.d. Web. 20 October 2009. <http://www.gilderlehrman.org/teachers/module.php?module_id=331>.

"KNIGHTS OF LABOR,." 2009. History.com. 21 Oct 2009, http://www.history.com/encyclopedia.do?articleId=213962.

"TRADE UNIONS IN THE UNITED STATES,." 2009. History.com. 21 Oct 2009, http://www.history.com/encyclopedia.do?articleId=224387.

"robber baron." Merriam-Webster Online Dictionary. 2009.

Davis, Kenneth C. *Don't Know Much About History*. New York: Crown Publishers, Inc., 1990. Print.

Zieger, Robert H. and Gilbert J. Gall. *The Twentieth Century American Workers, American Unions*. 3rd ed. Baltimore: Johns Hopkins University Press, 2002. Print.

"UNION FACTS." 2009. aflcio.org 11 October 2009. <www.aflcio.org/aboutus/faq/>

Freeman, Sholnn. "Union Membership Up Slightly in 2007" WashingtonPost.com 26 January 2008. Web. 20 October 2009.

Whoriskey, Peter. "American Union Ranks Grow After Bottoming Out." WashingtonPost.com. 29 January 2009. Web. 26 October 2009.

Decay in Today's Economic Climate and Marketplace

Sherk, James. "Auto Bailout Ignores Excessive Labor Costs." Heritage.org. 19 November 2009. Web. 22 October 2009.

General Motors. For Third Consecutive Year, GM Sells More Than 9 Million Vehicles Globally. Detroit: GM, 23 January 2008. Web.

Booth, David. "US $38.78 Loss Not That Bad." Financialpost.com. 29 February 2009. Web. 1 September 2009. <http://www.financialpost.com/scripts/story.html?id=8ff0e916-38cf-4e74-bef6-c76d4b8a6678&k=19623>

Michigan State. *Office of the Governor. 2007 Economic Report of the Governor*. Lansing: State of Michigan. 2007. Print.

"TOYOTA'S PROFIT BOOSTED BY EMERGING MARKETS." 2008. MSNBC.com 5 February 2008. <http://www.msnbc.msn.com/id/23008016/>

Webster, Larry. "GM in Crisis: 5 Reasons Why America's Largest Car Company Teeters on the Edge." PopularMechanics.com 18 November 2008. <http://www.popularmechanics.com/automotive/new_cars/4292379.html>

Taylor, Alex III. "Behind Ford's Scary $12.7 Billion Loss." CNNMoney.com. 26 January 2007. Web. 27 October 2009. <http://money.cnn.com/2007/01/26/news/companies/pluggedin_taylor_ford.fortune/index.htm>

Sherk, James. "Auto Bailout Ignores Excessive Labor Costs" *Webmemo* #2135. 19 November 2008.Web. 27 September 2009. <http://www.heritage.org/Research/Economy/wm2135.cfm>

"BRIEF HISTORY" 2009. OPEC.org. 11 September 2009.
<http://www.opec.org/aboutus/>

Haglund, Rick. "GM Asks for Federal Help in Wake of Auto Industry Sales Carnage." *Grand Rapids Press*. 3 November 2008. Print. 26 October 2009.

Gustafson, Sven. "Analysts: GM Moves Jeopardize Research and Development Innovation." MichiganBusinessReview.com. 4 November 2009. Web. 26 October 2009.

Barry T. Hirsch, "Union Coverage and Profitability Among U.S. Firms," *The Review of Economics and Statistics*, Vol. 73, No. 1 February 1991, pp. 69-77. Web. 1 October 2009.

Bergeron, Peter. Union Proof, Indianapolis: DogEar, 2008
<http://www.unionproof.com>

"THE COST OF UNIONIZATION." 2009. Projectionsinc.com. 26 October 2009.
<http://www.projectionsinc.com/article_cost_unionization.html>

Furchtgott-Roth, Diana. "Union Bigs Get the Best Deals: A Sour Labor Day Lesson on Pensions." NYDailyNews.com. 7 September 2009. Web. 11 October 2009.

Mooney, Kevin. "Union Pension Plans Hurt Workers, Study Shows." WashingtonExaminer.com. 9 September 2009. Web. 11 October 2009.

Freeman, Richard B., "Union Wage Practices and Wage Dispersion Within Establishments." *Industrial and Labor Relations Review*. Vol. 36, No. 1. October 1982.

United States Department of Labor, Bureau of Labor Statistics. *Employer Costs for Employee Compensation*—June 2009 Washington, D.C.: United States Department of Labor, 10 September 2009. Print.

Sherk, James. "What Unions Do: How Labor Unions Affect Jobs and the Economy" *The Backgrounder* #2275. 21 May 2009.Web. 27 September 2009.
<http://www.heritage.org/research/labor/bg2775.cfm>

Barry T. Hirsch and David A. Macpherson, "Union Membership and Coverage Database from the Current Population Survey: Note," Industrial and Labor Relations Review, Vol. 56, No. 2, January 2003, pp. 349-54. (in pdf)

Kramarz, Francis. *Outsourcing, Unions and Wages: Evidence from Data Matching Imports, Firms and Workers*. 19 October 2006. Web. 22 October 2009.

Lee, David and Alexandre Mas, *Long-Run Impacts of Unions on Firms: New Evidence from Financial Markets*, 1961-1999 National Bureau of Economic Research *Working Paper* No. 14709, February 2009.

Hirsch, Barry. *Labor Unions and the Economic Performance of U.S. Firms*. Kalamazoo: Upjohn Institute for Employment Research. 1991. Print.

Krol, Robert and Shirley Svorny. "Unions and Employment Growth: Evidence from State Economic Recoveries." *Journal of Labor Research*. Vol. 18, No. 3 Summer, 2007. Print.

Vedder, Richard K. and Lowell E. Gallaway. *Out of Work: Unemployment and Government in the Twentieth-Century America.* New York. New York University Press. 1993. Print.

Elliot, Philip. "Obama Tells Autoworkers His Policies Help Them." news.yahoo.com. 15 September 2009. Web. 15 September 2009.

Valdes-Dapena, Peter. "After cash for clunkers, higher prices" CNNMONEY.com. 27 August 2009. Web. 15 September 2009.

Cole, Harold L. and Lee E. Ohanian, "New Deal Policies and the Persistence of the Great Depression: A General Equilibrium Analysis" *Journal of Political Economy,* Vol. 112, No. 4 (August 2004), pp. 779-816.

"CARD CHECK: LEARN THE BASICS." 2009. USChamber.com. 22 October 2009. <http://www.uschamber.com/wfi/cardcheckbasics.htm#penalties>

The Strong-Arm of a Union

Renik, Lindsay. "Labor and Business Spend Big on Looming Unionization Issue." OpenSecrets.org 26 February 2009. Web. 3 September 2009. <http://www.opensecrets.org/news/2009/02/labor-and-business-spend-big-o.html>

Obama, Barack. *The Audacity of Hope.* New York: Crown Publishers, 2006. Print.

Renik, Lindsay. "Labor and Business Spend Big on Looming Unionization Issue." OpenSecrets.org 26 February 2009. Web. 3 September 2009. <http://www.opensecrets.org/news/2009/02/labor-and-business-spend-big-o.html>

Renik, Lindsay. "Unions Funded Nominee's Work as Congresswoman." OpenSecrets.org. 19 December 2008. Web. 3 September 2009.

Nicholas, Peter (2009-01-30). "Republicans Want Labor Nominee to Stop Lobbying for "Card Check" Bill". LATimes.com 5 February 2009. Web. 19 October 2009. <http://www.latimes.com/news/nationworld/nation/la-na-nominees30-2009jan30,0,5539680.story.>

Fletcher, Michael A. "Solis Cleared for Senate Confirmation Later Today." WashingtonPost.com 24 February 2009. Web. 20 October 2009. <http://voices.washingtonpost.com/44/2009/02/24/solis_cleared_for_senate_confi.html.>

A House Divided

Hunt, Albert. "Infighting is Blunting Labor's Clout." NYTimes.com. 6 September 2009. Web. 17 September 2009.

Robert J. Lalonde, Gerard Marschke, and Kenneth Troske, "Using Longitudinal Data on Establishments to Analyze the Effects of Union Organizing Campaigns in the United States," *Annales d' Economie et de Statistique*, Vol. 41-42 (January- June 1996), pp. 155-185

Petruno, Tom. "Amid Dismal Job Market, Americans Grow Warier of Unions." LATimes.com. September 7, 2009. Web. 18 September 2009.

Jarmen, Max. "Grocery Workers: Unified Front?" *The Arizona Republic.* 24 November 2009. Print.

Employee Free Choice Act

EFCA, H.R. 1409, S. 560

S. 560, 111th Congress

"THE FACTS: WHAT FREEDOM TO JOIN UNIONS MEANS TO AMERICA'S WORKERS AND THE MIDDLE CLASS." Aflcio.org. 2008. <http://www.aflcio.org/joinaunion/voiceatwork/efca/>

Sherk, James. "EFCA Authorizes Government Control of 4 Million Small Businesses." *Web Memo #2341.* (2009): Heritage Foundation. Web. 1 September 2009.

Packer, Katie. "Unions Must Stop Supporting Legislation That Kills Jobs." FoxNews.com 4 September 2009. Web. 16 September 2009.

Renik, Lindsay. "Labor and Business Spend Big on Looming Unionization Issue." OpenSecrets.org. 26 February 2009. Web. 1 October 2009. <http://www.opensecrets.org/news/2009/02/labor-and-business-spend-big-o.html>

Cooper, Rory. "Employee "No" Choice Act: Increasing the Fed's Role Again." Heritage.org 10 March 2009. Web. 1 September 2009. <http://www.heritage.org/Press/FactSheet/fs0014.cfm>

Lee, David and Alexandre Mas, *Long-Run Impacts of Unions on Firms: New Evidence from Financial Markets*, 1961-1999 National Bureau of Economic Research Working Paper No. 14709, February 2009.

Renshaw, Jarrett. "Union Troubled by Eagle Scout Project in Allentown." www.mccall.com. 15 November 2009. Web. 14 December 2009.

Coalition for a Democratic Workplace. *New Poll: Union Members Oppose Big Labor's Card Check.* Washington, D.C.: Coalition for a Democratic Workplace, 26 January 2009. Web. 17 September 2009.

Vecsey, Laura. *"Card Check" Fight Focuses on Jobs*, Pay. PennLive.com. 8 September 2009. Web. 17 September 2009.

A Success Story

Walton, Sam *Made in America: My Story* New York: Doubleday, 1992. Print.

"ABOUT US" www.walmartstores.com n.d. Web. 11 September 2009. <http://walmartstores.com/AboutUs/>

Delevingne, Lawrence. "2009 Most Admired Companies" Fortune Magazine. N.d. Web. 11 September 2009. <http://money.cnn.com/magazines/fortune/mostadmired/2009/snapshots/2255.html>

Helm, Burt and Moira Herbst. "Fed-Ex's Anti-Union Drive." Businessweek.com. 9 June 2009. Web. 8 December 2009.

"WHY IS ABC OPPOSED TO UNION-ONLY PLAS?" abc.org. n.d. web. 8 December 2009.

Wal-Mart. In Fourth Area, *UFCW Union Leaders Block Election*. Bentonville: Wal-Mart, n.d. Web. 20 October 2009.
<http://walmartstores.com/FactsNews/NewsRoom/4198.aspx>

Wal-Mart. *"Wal-Mart Associates to UFCW: :Leave Us Alone!"* Bentonville: Wal-Mart, n.d. Web. 20 October 2009.
<http://walmartstores.com/FactsNews/NewsRoom/4377.aspx>

Maher, Kris and Ann Zimmerman. *"Union Intensifies Efforts to Organize Workers at Wal-Mart."* WSJ.com. 17 April 2009. Web. 13 September 2009.
<http://online.wsj.com/article/SB123992564986427357.html>

The Job Builder

Fowler, Bree. "GM to End Controversial 'Job Bank' Monday." abcnews.com Associated Press, 28 January 2009. Web. 20 October 2009.

George, Thomas. "Rice Won't Forget His Former Partner in the Sublime" NYTimes.com. The New York Times, 11 September 1994. Web. 26 August 2009.

Harter, James K., Frank L. Schmidt and Theodore L. Hayes. "Business-Unit-Level Relationship Between Employee Satisfaction, Employee Engagement, and Business Outcomes: A Meta-Analysis. *American Psychological Association, Inc.* Vol. 87. No. 2 (2002): 268-279. Print

"LABOR RELATIONS" www.dol.gov. n.d. Web 15 December 2009.

Isoidore, Chris. "GM, UAW Reach Cost Cutting Deal" cnn.money.com 28 January 2009. Web. 5 September 2009.
<http://money.cnn.com/2009/01/28/news/companies/gm_uaw_jobsbank/index.htm>.

Lewes, G.H.

Lincoln, Abraham. "Annual Address Before the Wisconsin State Agricultural Society, at Milwaukee, Wisconsin, September 30, 1859." *The Complete Works of Abraham Lincoln*, vol. 5. Eds. John G. Nicolay and John Hay. New York: Francis D. Tandy Company, 1894.

Schwartz, Larry. *Montana Was Comeback Kid* http://www.ESPN.com,

n.d. Web. 19 October 2009
<http://espn.go.com/sportscentury/features/00016306.html>.

Swan, Gary, "BECKETT SPORTS HEREOS: JOE MONTANA." http://www.thedebster.com. N.p. n.d. Web. 19 October 2009.
<http://www.thedebster.com/nflstats.html>.

www.cisco.com 2008. Web. 3 August 2009.

www.money.CNN.com. Fortune 2009. Web. 15 August 2009
<http://money.cnn.com/magazines/fortune/bestcompanies/2009/full_list/index.html>.

Right-to-Work States

Lindsly, Rand. Quotation # 23111

"capitalism." *Merriam-Webster Online Dictionary*. 2009.Merriam-Webster Online. 3 November 2009 <http://www.merriam-webster.com/dictionary/capitalism>

Hooker, Richard. "Capitalism." WSU.edu. 14 July 2009. Web. 3 November 2009.

Bernanke, Ben. *"The Level and Distribution of Economic Well-Being."* Greater Omaha Chamber of Commerce. Omaha, Nebraska. 6 February 2007. Address.

"BOARD MEMBERS." Federalreserve.gov. 23 October 2009. Web. 2 November 2009.

"HOME." Nrtw.org. Web. 2 November 2009.

Fischer, Mark and Robert P. Hunter. "First Amendment Challenges to Forced Union Membership." Mackinac.org. 7 June 2000. Web. 8 December 2009. <http://www.mackinac.org/article.aspx?ID=2914>

"DO YOU LIVE IN A RIGHT TO WORK STATE?" http://nrtw.org/ n.d. Web 15 December 2009.

"RIGHT TO WORK LAW AND LEGAL DEFINITION." Definitions.uslegal.com. Web 2 November 2009.

"RIGHT TO WORK STATES: NORTH CAROLINA." www.nrtw.org. n.d. Web. 11 December 2009. <http://www.nrtw.org/c/ncrtwlaw.htm>

Larson, Reed. *Stranglehold: How Union Bosses Have Hijacked Our Government*. Ottawa: Jameson Books, Inc., 1999. Print.

Williams, David A. *Right-to-work Laws: Is There Economic Justification for Them?*

Graham, Robert S. The Robert S. Graham Foundation. 2009.

"Texas v. Ohio." Editorial. Wall Street Journal Online. 3 March 2008. Web. 7 December 2009. <http://online.wsj.com/article/SB120450306595906431.html>

"ABOUT US." Aflcio.org. n.d. Web. 16 November 2009.

Lower Taxes = Higher Revenue

Larson, Reed. *Stranglehold: How Union Bosses Have Hijacked Our Government*. Ottawa: Jameson Books, Inc., 1999. Print.

Morgan, Iwan. "Seeing Red: The Budget Deficit – Past, Present and Future." Hnn.com. 19 November 2009. Web. 1 November 2009. <http://www.hnn.us/articles/120032.html>

Laffer, Arthur B. and Jonathan Moore. *Rich States, Poor States* Princeton University Press. 2008. Print.

Top Corporate Tax Rates. Chart. Heritage Foundation: Taxes: Yesterday, Today and Tomorrow. April 2009.

Taking Back the Dream

"All that is necessary…" www.quotationsbook.com. N.d. Web. 10 November 2009. http://quotationsbook.com/quote/46369/

"The day soldiers stop…" <http://www.leadership-tools.com/leadership-quotes.html> N.d. web. 8 December 2009.

"Leadership is the activity…" <http://www.leadership-tools.com/leadership-quotes.htm> N.d. web. 8 December 2009.

Kichen, Steve. "Made in America." Forbes.com. 28 May 2009. Web. 17 November 2009. <http://www.forbes.com/2009/05/28/american-manufacturing-factories-business-makers_land.html>

Popular Mechanics, November 18, 2008 by Larry Webster re: David Cole quote and $2,000 legacy costs <http://www.popularmechanics.com/automotive/new_cars/4292379.html>

Flint, Jerry. *"They Can Build Them; Why Can't We?"* Forbes.com. 28 May 2009. Web. 16 November 2009.

Ewalt, David M. and Michael Noer, eds. *"What is the American Dream?"* forbes.com 22 March 2007. Web. 30 July 2009. <http://www.forbes.com/2007/03/20/american-dream-oped-cx_de_dream0307_0322dream_land.html>

Kennedy, John F. "Address at Rice University on the Nation's Space Efforts." Houston, Texas. 12 September 1962. Address. <http://www.jfklibrary.org/Historical+Resources/Archives/Reference+Desk/Speeches/JFK/003POF03SpaceEffort09121962.htm>

Adams, James Truslow. *The Epic of America.* 1931. Safety Harbor: Simon Publications, 2001. Print.